NORMAN YOUNG is Professor of
Systematic Theology, Queens College,
University of Melbourne, Australia. He is
a graduate of Queens College, University
of Melbourne; and of The Theological
School, Drew University, where he
received his Ph.D. from the Graduate
School. He was Deputy Master, King's
College, University of Queensland, and
held visiting professorships at Princeton
Theological Seminary and Yale Divinity
School.

Creator, Creation
and Faith

BOOKS BY NORMAN YOUNG

PUBLISHED BY THE WESTMINSTER PRESS

Creator, Creation and Faith

History and Existential Theology:
The Role of History in the Thought of Rudolf Bultmann

CREATOR, CREATION
AND
FAITH

Norman Young

THE WESTMINSTER PRESS
PHILADELPHIA

Z 1 3
Y 8 6
C. 2

BT
695
.Y68

203044

Library of Congress Cataloging in Publication Data

Young, Norman James.
  Creator, creation and faith.

  Includes bibliographical references and index.
  1. Creation. I. Title.
BT695.Y68   213   76–10324
ISBN 0–664–21334–0

To Graeme and Paul
who share the joy
of God's good creation

Contents

Preface

What difference does it make if we believe in God as creator? How does it affect the way people live in the world in the present and face the future?

This book is a modest approach to those questions. Modest, because it sets out not so much to break new scholarly ground as to help those who may not be experts in the field to see the significance of some recent scholarly work. In particular it is concerned to show how the conclusions drawn by some biblical scholars and theologians during the last few decades have profound implications for how we are to live our lives in the world and to tackle the overwhelming problems that confront us. An approach, because the range of bibilical themes and theological formulations is far from exhaustive, and many would have preferred other approaches and theologians to the ones I have considered. The choice was very much a personal one, for those that do appear are the ones that have, more than any others, shaped my own thinking and attitudes so far. Given more time and opportunity for research and discussion, the process theologians would certainly have been next on the list, and I would like to think that the methodology suggested here could be usefully extended to other doctrines and theological approaches.

My thanks are due to a great many people. To Bernhard Anderson who first showed me that the results of biblical criticism have significance far beyond the confines of scholarly expertise, and whose book *Creation versus Chaos* opened new horizons; to Claus Westermann for his influential work on the doctrine of creation and to H. Richard Niebuhr for the methodology suggested in his *Christ and*

Culture; to the University of Otago (Dunedin, New Zealand) for inviting me to give the Thomas Burns Lectures in 1973 when this book began to take shape, and to the faculty and students at Knox College who received me so warmly; to my students at the United Faculty of Theology, Melbourne, and at the Divinity School at Yale University, who took my ideas apart and helped me put them together again; to the Principal and students at Wesley House, Cambridge, where most of the writing was done, and to the members of the Eucharistic Community at Armadale in Melbourne who gave me seclusion and hospitality for the final preparation of the manuscript; and to Lady Collins for her great interest in the Australian theological scene and for her encouragement over a number of years.

Queen's College, Melbourne,   N.J.Y.
February 1976.

1. Introduction:
Belief in God as Creator

How the world began hardly rates a mention in current religious debate, but the doctrine of creation does because it faces the much wider and livelier issues of God's relation to the world and of our present and future within it.

In many ways this seems an obvious place to start any serious thinking about the christian faith. The Old Testament begins with pictures of God creating, and whatever else varies in these Genesis accounts the work of the creator-God is at the focus of both. John's witness to the good news also begins with the creation, identifying Jesus Christ with God's creative word that was from the beginning. The most ancient and widely accepted creeds also open with the 'Maker of Heaven and Earth'[1] and as time went on influential theological systems still began with the doctrine of creation. The first part of Calvin's *Institutes*, for instance, deals with the knowledge of God as creator. The first of the Thirty-nine Articles also asserts belief in the 'Maker and Preserver of all things both visible and invisible', and when John Wesley revised the Articles for use by Methodists that clause remained in place. The Westminster divines, as might be expected, broke with tradition at this point as at so many others, giving pride of place to the Holy Scriptures. Nevertheless, they had their own way of underlining the importance of belief in God as sovereign over all creation – they allowed it in at second place, edging the famous clause on predestination into third position.

Those whose ears are more tuned to the present century will certainly have received the Barthian message. His *Church*

Dogmatics, which ran to a dozen volumes by ordinary standards of reckoning,[2] gave more space to the doctrine of creation than to any other, amounting to some two thousand three hundred pages in English. Barth was a great enough man to see the irony in this, that so many words should come from one who insisted so strongly on the priority of God's word over human words, and in later prefaces he joked about the length and time involved. He may even have appreciated what I once saw in a University bookstore – the *Dogmatics* being sold at $2.20 per pound.

Nevertheless, when all of these have been put together, all the biblical references, the controversies, creeds, confessions, the systems of past and present, all may yet amount to no more than satellite theology – up in the air, going round in circles, and liable to disintegrate when brought down to earth. The doctrine of creation may well have a place in the history of theology or in theoretical systems of belief, but has it anything to say to human life in the present? What difference does believing in God as creator make? What are the living implications of having one kind of belief about creation and not another? These are the questions I want to bring to bear on the subject, and they give shape and direction to the discussion that follows in this book.

Such an approach takes account of the fact that most of the debates that have raged in this century over the doctrine of creation have raised life and death issues for those involved, and consequently spread far beyond academic circles. However, fervour does not guarantee a valid conclusion. Often a quick solution was sought by a division of interests, but in the long run the problems returned, like the broken broomstick of the sorcerer's apprentice, to give more trouble than before. To take four examples:

1. Belief in God as creator provided the focus for the *science-religion debates* of the earlier part of this century.

Whether the Bible could be believed at all ('If you can't believe the Genesis accounts of creation what *can* you believe . . . ?'), whether scientific conclusions had to stand under ecclesiastical veto, whether being a Christian and accepting a scientific world-view were mutually exclusive, all were argued in terms of evolution versus creation.

This may now seem to be over and done with, no more than a reminder of past folly, and where the argument still drags on it may be discounted as a bizarre although still destructive relic of the past, like a voodoo charm whose malevolence remains for those who take it seriously. But that, I think, is an over-simplification. Of course the original battle ought to be finished because it took place in terrain that neither side had properly reconnoitred. Both sides claimed too much, and the weapons they rolled out to back up their claims did more damage to themselves than to the enemy. The creation stories in Genesis, for instance, did not and do not depend for their value on their acceptability as cosmologies, and to have a different theory of how the world began is not to deny what the Genesis accounts affirm about God, the world and mankind. Therefore theologians were claiming too much for the Bible when they demanded that the scientific accounts of the origins of man and the world should fit some superior version that the Bible offered.[3] Scientists for their part went too far when they insisted that their theories destroyed the need for God and left no basis for belief in him as creator. It was as though the defenders of the faith, working from a faulty reading of the biblical blue-prints, built a replica of the creator-God at which scientists then proceeded to fire. The world shook at the bombardment of claim and counter-claim, but although neither side knew it at the time, the target was only a decoy. The creator-God was not in the firing line at all.[4]

However, having acknowledged all that, should we now conclude that there is nothing worth fighting about, no ground on which battle should be joined? Are we right to perpetuate between science and religion a 'frostily amicable bi-lateral quarantine'?[5]

There is certainly a widely-held view of the world, called 'scientific', that does seem to pose more than a pseudo-challenge to the understanding of God as one who not only brings into being but also sustains and opens the way to the radically new. It makes claims not only about how things began but also about how they continue, and posits a universe of cause and effect that allows for no kind of being or power transcendent to it and no newness apart from the range of possibilities already resident within the system itself. Is belief in a creator-God then possible at all? That is still a live question of more than academic interest, with implications for the way we view the world, try to live in it and plan for its future.

During the last few decades attempts have been made, by proposing a neat division of interests, to avoid the question rather than answer it. The scientist, it is said, is welcome to the realm of nature; the theologian ought to stay in the field of history where he should have been all along. Accordingly, when Christians affirm belief in God as creator they do not intend to say anything about the natural world of cause and effect. They are really only speaking of man and his history,[6] and then, according to one mutation of this approach, not about the history of the world and the nations but only about one's own personal history. But this reduction of the scope of the doctrine of creation from the cosmic to the existential, or from the natural to the historical, turns out to be a double failure. It relinquishes a vital component of faith without gaining immunity from attack in the process. The attack continues because someone who is unable to accept the idea of God's breaking into the cause-and-effect of nature is no more likely to accept his intrusion into history, whether that is the history of the nations or the history of the self. The question of the transcendence of God and of the possibilities open in the world for transformation or radical renewal remains unanswered.

In the unsuccessful attempt to avoid the problem this nature-history distinction runs into another one. To over-emphasize the historical dimension of the christian faith and to interpret the doctrines of creation and redemption solely in terms of historical drama leaves the world without God and without responsible human concern. This diminishes God by reducing the area of his concern, for what kind of God is he who does everything for the salvation of man but nothing for the world which is his home? It also limits the scope for human response to and celebration of the creative goodness of God, and can lead to a negative assessment of the natural world and of human participation in this, opening the way to exploitation of nature and even to sanctifying this attitude as proper service to God.

2. Events in Germany in the nineteen-thirties confirmed that the doctrine of creation is of more than antiquarian and theoretical interest, as it provided a focal point for the struggle within the Church and between *the Church and the Nazis.*

Removed as we are from the context of that struggle and looking back across forty years, the matters under theological dispute may seem remote and abstract. Does God reveal himself in nature as well as in history? Do we preach what we know of him in nature and history? Do the orders of creation reflect fallen human nature? Should creation or christology be the starting-point for theology and ethics? Those questions seem more appropriate to seminary textbooks than to national conflict, yet they were the questions discussed at Barmen and whose answers consolidated the Confessing Church's tenacious opposition to Hitler. These questions surfaced in the life and death struggle because the Nazis had revived the old pagan mythology of blood and soil, race and nation as a rallying-point for the people. Old

Germanic folk-myths were blended with some ingredients from the philosophies of Hegel and Nietzsche and set to the music of Wagner in order to fire imagination and enthusiasm. At the core of all this was the assertion that the creative power, or life-force, is manifest in the folk, the race and the nation, and, thus reinforced, patriotic fervour swept away all appeals to logic and reason. Christians were called on to endorse this patriotic myth by asserting that God is at work in the history of the nation, and that in the natural forces giving vitality to the nation God's creative power is there to be experienced and shared.

At the beginning there were many who were ready to answer the call, and from the secure vantage-point of hindsight it is easy to express shock and surprise. We ought to do neither. What is really more surprising, given the long history of the alliance between the governing powers of a nation and its churches, is that so many did come so strongly to reject it. Apart from the fact that with very few exceptions churches in all countries have supported the government, particularly in times of national crisis, Germans in the nineteen-thirties saw plenty of signs of national renewal that could be interpreted as a kind of new creation. Out of the chaos of industrial unrest and political instability the Nazis were bringing order. Out of the despair carried over from the defeat of the previous war there was growing hope. Out of the weakness, disillusionment and aimlessness of the youth there was evidence of rising strength, idealism and purpose. Add a not unfamiliar readiness of Christians to search for God at work in the secular as well as in the ecclesiastical realm and all the prerequisites were there for Christian participation in nation-building. 'Get where the action is; join God in his work in the world' is a cry heard often enough since then in many of the Western and most of the third world countries, so we should be able to appreciate its impact on Christians in Nazi Germany.

It was only when the purges became increasingly violent,

when the Church itself was subjected to restriction and government control and when the persecution of Jews became more and more severe that Christian opposition began to solidify. The theological ground for that opposition was the insistence that the second article of the creed should be the interpreter of the first. While it is true that God is creator and does reveal himself in nature and history, what is genuinely of God and therefore genuinely creative can be recognized only by beginning with Jesus Christ. In him is seen the power of God at work. His history is the history of the authentically creative life. His was the way of new creation. He is the lord, the leader, and the validity of the leadership of any earthly Führer is to be measured against his.[7]

All this was forty years ago, but far from over and done with. This appeal to recognize the creative work of God in the world and to share the power of his new creation is very much alive, and the role of the Church and of Christians in nation-building is increasingly a matter for debate and action. The responsibility of the Church's members and leaders to support, criticize, revolt against or stay aloof from national policies and actions has never been a more critical issue than now. People living under totalitarian régimes of right or left, in democracies or nominally christian countries, in the first, second or third worlds may find the pressure coming at different points, but it comes with equal intensity.

In the nineteen-thirties a separation of God's revelation from the history of the nation provided the basis for opposition to an evil régime, but can the restriction of God's revelation to the sacred biblical history provide answers in the present situation? Does the separation of holy history from ordinary history, which the Confessing Church used to refute the claim that the Third Reich was God's new creation, also refute every claim to discern God's presence in the life of any nation? Does this mean that his work of re-creation can never be identified in the struggle for liberation or in the search for peace? Or is all this only a partial reading of the relation between God and his creation, expedient for the emergency situation in Nazi Germany but in effect limiting God's sovereign care, restricting the area of responsible human obedience, and, since providing only for negative political judgements, allowing initiative to be taken only for secular reasons?

3. This brings us to a third familiar line of theological argument that proposes much the same separation – the so-called *secularization theme.*

This is a very imprecise term, best understood by citing key ideas of its main proponents. Arend van Leeuwen in his *Christianity in World History*[8] claimed that it was the Judeo-christian view of God as creator that made possible the modern world-view, and, as a consequence, scientific and technological progress. To believe in God as creator implies that the world is neither divine nor evil, so that people are now set free from superstitious fear of punishment for inter-fering with the gods or unleashing the demons as they make for themselves a place in the world. We can therefore probe, experiment and modify without being afraid of reprisals. Only when God was thus seen as transcendent creator was the world made genuinely available to the human race – so went the theme echoed in a hundred books and in a hundred thousand pulpits.

But is it true? And, if it is, should we cheer or hang our heads in shame? If it is true then faith in God as creator in-vited not only praise for laying the foundation for techno-logical progress but also blame for opening up the way to ecological disaster, as more than one writer has pointed out to the discomfort of christian apologists trying to give Christianity credit for science's unacknowledged debt.

This, once again, is a vital issue affecting everyone's future, and those who look at it in christian perspective see the close connection with the doctrine of creation. And once again the problems involved are magnified by the technique of separation, this time separation between creator and creation. But is this separation justified? Is it just this separation that makes Christianity the most anthropocentric religion the world has known and therefore the main contributor to the destruction of the environment?[9] Does the lack of respect for nature and the environment stem from the doctrine of creation or from a perversion of it? Will the problem be overcome when the doctrine is made to reflect a continuity between the creator and the creation rather than a hiatus, a God who is organic to rather than sovereign over the world?[10] These questions will be taken up again when more attention has been given to the biblical themes and alternative theological approaches to them.

4. The *theology of hope*, with Jürgen Moltmann as its main spokesman, has also directed attention to the doctrine of creation. In the nineteen-sixties, in contrast to the prevailing concentration on the past mighty acts of God or the present saving acts of existential history, Moltmann proposed an orientation toward the future and the life of mankind in the world. Interpreting the biblical witness to God primarily as one who promises, Moltmann has consistently called for an interpretation of doctrine based on the expectation of that which has yet to come, and therefore an understanding of new creation becomes all-important. This amounts to much more than a shift in abstract theological concepts; it becomes a manifesto for social involvement. Influenced as he was by the Marxist views of Ernst Bloch, Moltmann does not allow orientation toward the future to become an enticing dream that helps us to put up with the present as it is. It becomes the motivation for present action. The vision of what should be in the future, far from helping us to tolerate the present, makes it intolerable. It is precisely the contrast between things as they are now and the preview of new cre-

ation glimpsed in Christ that calls for radical action, both in the Church which has distorted and domesticated the new creation and in the world which cries out for its fulfilment.

But should this radical action take the form of revolution? Perhaps revolution is the wrong *word*. Moltmann himself suggests 'provolution' because it avoids the idea of revolving and the 'myth of the eternal return' which see creation as no more than reinstatement of the old. Perhaps it is also the wrong *course*. Are revolutionary movements part of God's new creation in which Christians should be involved, or are they a descent into chaos which must therefore be resisted by the preservation of law and order? Or have they nothing to do with the redeeming and re-creative power of God which is directed to another level of reality, that of the human spirit?

These introductory paragraphs have identified some themes in contemporary theological discussion and some features of social concern that come together and focus on the doctrine of creation. In each case there were important questions that call for further elucidation of the creator-creature relationship before any answers can be attempted. More than once reference was made to 'the biblical witness', but this was not meant to imply that there is one biblical view of creation. There is biblical witness to God as creator, but it is varied, and account must be taken of this variation. There is also a variety of ways in which the biblical material may be interpreted. There are different methods of approach, different questions that can be put, different ways of putting the questions, different frames of reference, and all these result in conclusions that differ both in the way they interpret doctrine and in the kind of action that they call for.

In what follows there will therefore be two main sections and a conclusion. In the first the inter-related biblical themes of creation, fall and new creation will be identified, and in the second we shall look at what happens when these themes are approached in different ways and interpreted within four theological frameworks represented by Barth, Tillich, Bultmann and Moltmann. The conclusion will consider implications in these approaches for living within the created world.

A. INTER-RELATED BIBLICAL THEMES

2. Creation and Genesis

The biblical witness to God as creator is varied and complex, and no attempt will be made here to take account of all of it, nor to debate critical questions in detail, as that lies outside the scope of this book. Instead, three major themes will be identified and some reflections made on them so that later on it will be possible to contrast the results of approaching these themes from different theological perspectives.

1. *The Place of the Creation Stories*

It is always tempting to rush straight to the question: 'What could they mean for us today?', bypassing the prior: 'What did they mean at the time?' But by avoiding the second question we lose the means of answering the first. While we may leave the more technical aspects of critical analysis to the experts, no approach to the early chapters of Genesis that wants to discover what they mean can afford to overlook the question of how they got there in their present form. That they were not part of the earliest Israelite tradition is now generally recognized, and while scholars disagree at many points there is still broad acceptance of major features of von Rad's pioneering account.[1]

Embedded in the Hexateuch are three similar statements of belief, in Deut. 26:5–9, Deut. 6:20–4, and Joshua 24:2–13. Von Rad identified these as very ancient creeds recited at cultic festivals and therefore retaining much the same form from the beginning of the oral tradition. Recent studies have disputed both their age and their cultic use, suggesting that their present form is a relatively late construction and that they were used mainly to persuade the people to continue to obey the terms of the covenant because the covenant-God had been so good to them. That they summed up the normative belief of the people, stretching back to earliest times is not, however, disputed, whatever views are held about when and for what purpose they gained their present form. They bear witness to God's calling of Abraham, giving him many descendants who wandered throughout the land until they went down into Egypt and settled there. There they increased in strength and number, but were later put in bondage. God gave them Moses, called them out of Egypt and led them through the wilderness to the promised land.

This expression of the faith of the people became the pattern for the literary construction of the Hexateuch, providing a framework which was filled out with material which was in circulation at about the time of Solomon. These sources used by the compiler, whom von Rad believed to be the Yahwist writer, were the innumerable stories of the people, some of which were then being written down for the first time, although many had already been written and some were parts of much larger collections. Some clearly came from other cultures, but by the time they found their present place they had already been assimilated to the Israelite tradition.

The original purpose of these narratives was, more often than not, to explain why the people did this or that, why here and not there, why at this time and not at that, why, for example, they worshipped where they did and in the way they did. However, when the Yahwist came to use these he seldom did so in order to answer the original question. He wove them into the sacred history and subjugated the original meaning to his new purpose.

A good illustration of this is the tower of Babel narrative

in Genesis 11. The story originally answered the question why people spoke different languages, and probably why some tower famous in antiquity was left half-finished. In the biblical framework it serves a different purpose. Now it marks the end of the primeval history in Genesis, the 'capstone' as von Rad calls it, the culmination of human evil-doing which concludes with God's judgement on the whole human race. It also marks the transition to the history of the people of Israel under God, for while, immediately after the Babel narrative, there is an abrupt narrowing down from God's dealing with humanity to his calling one man, this calling is for the sake of the whole so that salvation can be extended through the covenant people to 'all the families of the earth' (12:3). So the apposition of 'the comfortless story about the building of the tower' with 'the strangely new thing that follows, the election and blessing of Abraham',[2] is one example of the way that the writer has of remoulding the original so that it takes its place in the overall pattern of sacred history.

In all this there has so far been no mention of the creation stories in Genesis. That is because they were not part of this earliest tradition. Unlike the earliest christian creeds, the ancient Israelite declarations of faith made no reference to God as 'maker of heaven and earth'. They began with Abraham and the patriarchs because that is how Israel's experience of God began, and consequently the primary Genesis for Israel was the creation of the people from those who had been no people. That, from their own experience, was *creatio ex nihilo*. On the basis of this experience and belief the creative power of God was projected back to the beginning. He who was first recognized as creator and redeemer of Israel came to be affirmed as lord of all the nations, creator of all that is. Therefore, to the accounts of their own history with God there was added a pre-history, a prologue which was shaped to match the knowledge of God that had come through their history and which in turn was made to re-

inforce that history. The material that was used came from
the cultures of people around them which to some extent they
shared, but in using this material it was transformed so that
it became an authentic reflection of what Israel had come
to experience in her history – the creative power of the one
God.

2. *Some Implications*

Without discussing any further how the creation stories in
Genesis found their present form and place, *that* they were
shaped to become prologue to sacred history has some significant implications, four of which will be discussed here.

(a) The creation stories as they now appear in Genesis have
already been reinterpreted. They have not, of course, been
turned into pre-scientific cosmologies or into anthropological
or sociological descriptions of the earliest days of the human
race. They have been translated out of the religious milieu
in which they were originally formulated into the folk-
lore of the people of Israel, and finally into the form that
fitted the theological outlook of the Priestly writer and the
Yahwist.

This translation is, in a sense, 'demythologizing'.[3] The
stories have been taken out of the highly complicated mythological arena of warring deities, divine rivalries and human
servitude to the gods, and have been reinterpreted within the
life and thought of the people of Israel so that they speak to
the experience of that people. Therefore the term 'demythologizing' is appropriate because that is what Bultmann
intended in his widely debated project of New Testament interpretation – not to dispense with myth but to reinterpret
it so that the message could be clearly heard and thus be
able to evoke an existential response. Nevertheless the form
of the reinterpreted creation stories remains mythological.
How could it be anything else if God was the only witness
to his work of creation? But it was just this mythical form

which met the deepest needs of the people whose interest in beginnings was directed mainly toward gaining reassurance in the present. Commenting on this, Westermann writes:

> Myth belonged originally to the context of survival, an expression therefore of one's understanding of existence, of one's understanding of the existence of the threatened self (and this is precisely the goal at which the existential interpretation aims with its demythologizing). Reflection on Creation meant to rehearse, in the present world and in man's dangerous situation, the beginning, when what now is came to be . . . a reiteration of the reality by virtue of which the world continues to exist.[4]

When we now listen to the creation stories we therefore hear 'the final form of an address to his contemporaries of an author and theologian of the Israelite people in the tenth century before Christ'.[5] We also hear the undertones of the experience of a people who have come to know the creative power of God in their history, undertones which are resonant to the address of the biblical writer. At the same time we catch an echo of something that comes from an even more distant past, a memory of the dread and hope that belongs to the beginning of the human race.

Just how distant is the past from which that echo comes and how widespread are its common tones has only recently been recognized. Since the end of the last century, of course, similarities between the biblical creation stories and those of the Babylonian cuneiform texts had sparked off considerable debate. However, the debate was largely restricted to trying to establish, sometimes by research but more often by rhetoric, which accounts were original and which dependent, and to what extent one was superior to the others. More recent investigation has shown that the biblical texts and other Near Eastern ones with which they were usually compared were all part of a long tradition stretching back thousands of years in which similar creation motifs recurred in varying forms back to the most primitive narratives.

A comparison of the biblical stories with the well-known Babylonian *Enuma Elish*, and with parallel stories in Egyptian, Syrian and Canaanite culture, shows the particular form of the myths which developed within Israel's experience and the distinctive use made of these by the biblical writers. There has been, for instance, a transformation from an intricate saga of warring between the gods in which the creation of the world was a by-product to a more direct affirmation of the creation of the heavens and the earth by the deliberate and orderly act of the one God. There is a move from the moulding of pre-existent matter into the world to the act of creating something entirely new by divine fiat or word. The idea of the world as the substance of a god, alive or dead, gives way to that of a created world distinct and separate from its creator. There is also a move from the view of man as a relatively insignificant plaything or servant, whose existence is sometimes an afterthought and subject to the whim of the gods, to man as the culmination of God's deliberate and ordered creation.

It is worth noting here that there was also a process of demythologizing within Greek culture when the philosophers reinterpreted existing mythologies. The view of the world which resulted was, however, markedly different from that of the Genesis accounts, and this is worth pursuing a little further since Greek philosophy came later to have such considerable influence on christian understanding.

Historians of Greek literature and philosophy point out that there was no smooth progression from mythology to philosophy. Instead there were successive reinterpretations, and various views competed with one another, from the earliest phases of animism and nature-worship to the rather lighthearted anthropomorphism of Homer. There was a partial return to earlier superstition in Hesiod, but, as Burnet indicates, this was really a demythologizing:

The *Theogony* is an attempt to reduce all the stories about the gods into a single system, and system is necessarily fatal to so wayward a thing as mythology . . . The Olympic pantheon took the place of the old local gods in men's minds.[6]

It was just this pantheon and the view of man and the world that went with it that was subject to the further de-mythologizing of philosophers, notably Socrates and Plato. Socrates challenged the young to think again about the stories of the gods, those divine beings who were supposedly leading their own existence on the mountain but occasionally interfering capriciously with human life. He raised consequent questions about the life and future of the city and its citizens which invited rejection of the traditional bases for individual and community life. For this he was executed as an atheist, a charge levelled later at Christians because they too challenged existing belief in the gods.

Plato went beyond the Socratic kind of critical questioning of the myths, and his thought retains one major feature of the mythological outlook – the division between two worlds. He reinterpreted it, of course, so that what was the religious 'world of gods/world of men' structure became the philosophical 'world of reality/world of appearance', but the dualism remained. This was primarily a dualism of being but there was a corresponding epistemological dualism because each world had its appropriate mode of apprehension. Reality is apprehended by knowledge, appearance by opinion. Accordingly, the world in which we live, which is made up of the realm of nature that is given to us and the world of things that we make for ourselves, is a world of appearance and less than real. Everything that is here is a copy, or a copy of a copy, of the fully real, and is therefore necessarily distorted to some extent and thus less than perfect. Only those who have somehow escaped from the dark cave of the world of appearance into the bright sunlight of reality can know the truth, and, through this knowledge, live life as it should be lived.

This view which, as we shall see, runs counter to the mainstream of Hebrew thought, nevertheless provided an intellectual framework for interpreting the faith from very early in the christian era, and remains influential to the present day. While there may be few theologians who would claim to be Platonists, the language of prayer-book, hymnal and everyday piety, which have far more to do with shaping and expressing the faith of most christian people than have theological treatises, is shot through with the sense of the unreality, impermanence and imperfection of this world, in contrast to the real and abiding world of the spirit. The implications of this go beyond theory and stereotyped ways of talking about the here and the hereafter to the sphere of action, because each way of looking at the world has its own view of how we should live in it. What one decides to do as an individual and within the community depends on how important this world is taken to be, and on whether knowing what is good sufficiently guarantees doing it.

The reinterpretation or successive reinterpretations which led to the present form of the biblical creation stories took a different turn, avoiding the Platonic type of dualism. The world was not seen to be, as such, distorted, imperfect, or less than real. It is God's creation, created as he intended and therefore good. It is no inferior and relatively unreal world but one which God has made, setting man within it to live a fruitful and responsible life. It is true that things are not now as they should be, but not because from the beginning the world was imperfect, unreal or distorted. Even the forces of evil, which are certainly taken seriously and whose effects are vividly portrayed, are generally seen to be somehow dependent upon God for their continued existence.[7] Although there may be remnants of the mythology of chaos, the conflict between God and the evil forces is not eternal; it is confined to the era between the creation and consummation.

Therefore human hope for salvation is seen not in terms of escape from this unreal or perverse world, or from the body which binds us to it, but in terms of the creative power of God who transforms the world and human life within it.

(b) This reinterpretation of the myths which gave them their present form was 'historicizing'. They became, as we have seen, prologue to the salvation history of the people. The starting-point for faith was God's creative presence in that history, and so the creation stories were shaped in order to reflect that historical experience of the people. This has two consequences.

First, where there were similar creation-myths in other cultures they were used to celebrate the eternal cycle of the seasons associated with the great cosmic drama of death and renewal. In these celebrations the myths were more than stories about the distant past. They provided script and scenario for the cultic rites that enabled people themselves to become part of the annual renewal of creation. Through re-enactment the event itself was made present. ' "May he continue to conquer Tiamat and shorten her days!" the celebrant exclaimed. The combat, the victory and the creation took place at that very moment.'[8]

For Israel, however, the definitive cultic participation was in the drama of the people's history with God. The great events remembered and celebrated at the core of that history belonged to the present age of living memory, not to some dream-time before history nor to some mystical arena above history. Israel, of course, no less than her neighbours faced the uncertainties of the present and the terrors of an unknown future, but she looked for meaning not by exchanging the dissonance of history for the harmony of nature but by seeking within history the pattern of God's creative purpose.

Evidence of this transformation can be found, as a number of scholars have pointed out, in some of the Psalms. Psalm 24, for example, which is a Psalm for the autumn festival, begins by celebrating the creative power of the Lord ('The earth is the Lord's and all that is in it . . .') and might have been expected to go on and rejoice in the fruits of the season, but it does not. It goes on to proclaim that the king of glory is 'The Lord mighty in battle', so that attention quickly moves from the one who founded the earth to he who created and sustains his people.[9] Psalm 95 which, according to the Mishna, is a New Year Psalm, shows a similar preference for the historical. Unlike the Babylonian equivalents where the New Year is the occasion for celebrating the renewal of the nature cycle, the Psalm recited the beginning of the nation, pointing to the Exodus and setting the whole within the historical rhythm of God choosing, the people disobeying, God redeeming and renewing. A similar transposition is seen in the way the link between the Passover and the Canaanite festival of spring was broken by transforming the Passover into a celebration of the Exodus.

Second, later references in the Old Testament to God as creator deliberately link this to his mighty acts in history, with the emphasis falling on the historical experience of calling and saving the people rather than on 'maker of heaven and earth'. God is affirmed as creator in order to remind the people of the solemn nature of their calling and covenant, and to reassure them that he really is capable of saving them. Once again interest in God the creator of the world is made subservient to his creative acts within the history of the people. So, for instance, second Isaiah builds the components of Israel's vocation on the foundation of God's power, guaranteed by his having created the whole earth.

> Thus speaks the Lord who is God,
>> he who created the skies and stretches them out,
>> who fashioned the earth and all that grows in it,
> who gave breath to its people,

the breath of life to all who walk upon it:
I, the Lord, have called you with righteous purpose
and taken you by the hand;
I have formed you, and appointed you
to be a light to all peoples,
a beacon for the nations,
to open eyes that are blind,
to bring captives out of prison,
out of the dungeons where they lie in darkness

(42:5–7).

Similarly, Isaiah 51:15–16:

I am the Lord your God, the Lord of Hosts is my name.
I cleft the sea and its waves roared, that I might fix the
heavens in place and form the earth and say to Zion,
'You are my people.' I have put my words in your mouth
and kept you safe under the shelter of my hand.

(c) The creative work of God is not limited to the beginning
of either world or nation. Belief in God as the creator of all
things in the beginning was, as we have seen, derived from
experience of him in the history of the people. This creative
work was seen especially in his making a people of those who
had been no people, but, while this creative work was known
especially in the Exodus event, it was by no means restricted
to this. The continuing work of sustaining the people when
times were hard and saving them when threatened with destruction was seen to manifest the same creative power that
brought the world and the people into being in the first
place, and consequently God's saving acts are described over
and over again in images that recall both the primeval creation and the creation of the nation. This is particularly
evident in second Isaiah, as Bernhard Anderson has illustrated in a detailed chart.[10] In the new covenant passage in
Jeremiah, also, pictures of the two creations, of the people
and of the world, are superimposed, adding depth and

authenticating the word of God's continuing saving work, a work which is nothing less than new creation:

> The time is coming, says the Lord, when I will make a new covenant with Israel and Judah . . . These are the words of the Lord, who gave the sun for a light by day and the moon and the stars for a light by night, who cleft the sea and its waves roared; the Lord of Hosts is his name (Jer. 31:31, 35).

This passage is set in the context of the expectation of a new covenant and points to the culmination of God's creative work. Therefore, while the creative activity of God is not restricted to the beginning of things, neither is it seen as an endless succession of re-creative events. There was a beginning; there is the present; there will be an end. God who is the first shall also be the last. Just as the people projected their historical experience of God back to the beginning so they projected it forward to the end as well, and the consummation is therefore pictured both as new creation and new exodus. But more of that in a later chapter.

(d) The first three chapters of Genesis are an integral part of the wider literary unit, Genesis 1–11. This has been recognized for long enough by biblical scholars, but too often overlooked by theologians whom Westermann[11] takes to task for considering that for all doctrinal purposes the accounts of creation and fall are complete in chapters 1-3. Consequently, he maintains, once they have extracted the themes of creation and fall from these chapters they jump straight to the New Testament to match them up with the themes of redemption and new creation in Jesus Christ. If other material from Genesis is cited it is often only to illustrate, or to draw conclusions from, what is already understood from chapters 1-3. Such a leap, however, sidesteps two important considerations. First, the Genesis stories as they now come to us were concerned not so much with how the world, man and evil began in the first place as with elaborating their present relationship in the ongoing purpose of God. Stories about the past were used to illustrate a particular view of the present. Second, this is the theme of the first eleven chapters as a whole, and the later chapters add to this view; they do not merely elucidate what is in the earlier part. Therefore to stop at chapter 3, or to see chapters 4-11 as only drawing illustrative inferences from the first three, is to focus the theological spotlight on too narrow a range of biblical territory. At least half the picture is then out of sight.

It is clear, for example, that the flood narrative of chapters 6-9 stands in parallel with the first creation story in such a way that it adds to rather than simply reiterates the meaning of Genesis 1. In the first there is the picture of order emerging out of chaos through the creative word of God. In the account of the flood we see the created order all but engulfed once more by the watery chaos; not because, as in the earlier forms of the myth, the power of the creator-God is finely balanced against the powers constantly at war against him, but because his sovereign creative power is not unconditional. If the Priestly account of Genesis 1 is allowed to stand alone it could be concluded that God, having created the world and all that is in it, now ensures eternally its continuity. Not so, the flood narrative asserts. That the creator holds the creation in his hands is threat as well as promise, providing the basis for judgement as well as for salvation. The covenant at the end of the story assures preservation of the earth, but not from everlasting to everlasting. That belongs to God alone. The promise of preservation endures 'while the earth remains'; but as it had a beginning so it will come to an end.

In the same way, the doctrine of work is seen in full perspective only when Genesis 4:17–22 is added to the portrayal of work in 3:17–19. If the earlier verses are allowed to stand on their own then only one side of human work is seen – the way it reflects our fallen condition and imposes a constant and frustrating burden. Genesis 4:17–22, on the other hand, puts the positive side, showing that within the limits of creaturely existence it can be productive and indeed creative. The capacities to build, to care for the earth and to domesticate its creatures, to work its metals and to make music are all among God's good gifts to mankind. Work therefore shares in both curse and blessing, is both static and dynamic, can be an intolerable burden or the greatest joy, part of our rebellion against the creator or our participation in his creative work, and this equivocal nature of work is recognized only when Genesis 3 and 4 are put together to form the whole picture.

3. *Four Transitional Comments*

Some issues have been raised in this discussion which need some additional comment before they can be considered again, as they will be in Part B, from different theological perspectives.

(a) We have seen the way in which the transformation of the creation myths which led to their present form in Genesis eliminated features of the older mythologies, such as polytheism and nature-worship, which ran counter to the faith of Israel. It would be a mistake, however, to imagine that all the problems were solved, and in fact the problem of evil was, if anything, heightened when the hordes of warring deities were made to give way to the one all-sovereign creator. George Hendry, in a provocative address to the American Theological Society in 1971,[12] maintained that when the redactors shaped the creation stories in order to project back to the beginning their historical experience they did not take seriously enough the extent of the continuing struggle against the forces of evil. Isaiah and the Psalms retained the life and death dimensions of the continuing battle between creator and the chaotic forces, but the Priestly writer in particular obliterated the evidence of that battle. In a startling break with the customary praise for the sonorous tones and stately theology of Genesis 1, Hendry asserted:

> By this neat job of demythologization and naturalistic interpretation he changed the character of the creative act from a life and death struggle with a mysterious adversary to a smooth fiat of divine engineering . . . He depicted the divine creative act in such a sovereign unilateral way as an achievement of good and so completely erased all traces of resistance and opposition that the resultant picture was hard to reconcile with experience.[13]

Whether we go all the way with that estimate or not, there is no doubt that the more sovereignty is attributed to the good creator the greater the problem posed by the very existence of evil and its threatening force. Where did it come from in the first place, and why does God allow it to continue?

It may be, of course, that this is an insoluble problem and that theological attempts to account for the origin of evil necessarily fail because they reduce its mystery and therefore its profundity. It may also be that to treat evil as a 'problem to be solved' at all is entirely the wrong approach. Evil is not so much a problem to be solved as a threat to be faced and overcome. However, this does not really meet Hendry's point, for he is concerned not just with the theological problems bequeathed by the Priestly creation story but with the need to take seriously the full extent of the threatening forces of evil. If, as I have maintained with Westermann, the purpose of the creation stories was to talk about the beginnings in order to give reassurance about the present, this reassurance is less effective if it fails to see the full extent of the threat. Therefore the relationship between creation and evil needs to be explored not just in terms of man as sinner perverting the good order of creation, but of man as creature threatened by forces of total destruction that can be met and overcome only through the power of the creator-God.

(b) We have seen how important 'historicizing' was in the reinterpretation of the creation myths. We ought also to recognize that to over-emphasize this runs the danger of reducing drastically the scope of activity attributed to God, confining him to the stream of human history, even to one current within the stream.

To take the second point first. I am persuaded by scholars of the Old Testament that the chronology of belief was from God the creator of Israel to God the creator of heaven and earth. I am not persuaded that the creation stories are therefore important only as prologue to Israel's history, nor that Old Testament references to God as creator are important largely because they confirm his reliability as Israel's redeemer. They are important because they proclaim what they obviously do proclaim – God as creator of all mankind, Lord of all the nations – and the significance of that is not diluted either because it came later than belief in God as creator of Israel, or because it remained linked to that belief.[14] Israel at her worst may have restricted the concern of God as saviour to herself, but this was already recognized and denounced by the biblical writers themselves as an aberration. As the Old Testament makes clear, it was by being reminded that God was creator of all people and all nations that Israel was brought back to her senses. Therefore the order of belief, from God redeemer of Israel to creator of the world, must not be taken to reflect the priorities of God himself, as the object lesson to Jonah makes clear enough. Why should not God save Nineveh, that great city? He had after all created its people, and its cattle too! So the relationship between creator and redeemer becomes plain. God is redeemer because he is creator and is concerned for all his creation – that is primary. That he is effective redeemer because, since creator, he is powerful enough to redeem, is secondary. To affirm that God is creator is first of all to say why and whom he *does* save; only then is it to reassure us that he is *able* to save.

That brings us back to the first point. This emphasis on history can lead to a view of the natural order from which God has somehow been excluded. It is true that the focus of Israel's faith was the God who made historical covenant with his people, and that in the struggle against the fertility cults Israel stressed participation in salvation history rather than in nature cycle. It may also be true that 'one of the most important dates in the history of religion occurred when Israel transposed old nature festivals into commemorations of historical dates [manifesting] the power and deeds of God',[15] but it is going too far to conclude, as some have done, that the doctrine of creation deals only with history and has nothing to do with nature. From there it is a predictable if not necessary step to the view that since God is not involved with the world of nature then we can deal with it as we will, or that the command to subdue the earth is an open invitation to exploit it.

That, of course, is a travesty. Far from agreeing with those who blame the biblical tradition for the ecological crisis we should insist that it is a neglect or distortion of the biblical witness that precipitates the crisis. Nevertheless we must admit that one familiar form of 'biblical theology' that seeks to interpret everything in terms of salvation-history does open the way to that kind of distortion. So to my next comment.

(c) This 'historicizing' was not a complete transposition from nature to history. I do not mean by this just that there were some vestiges of nature-mythology that Israel overlooked – a fortunate oversight according to Richard Rubinstein who commented that 'the priests of ancient Israel never suffered Yahweh entirely to win his war against Baal, Astarte and Anath'.[16] Nor do I mean that there were some minor

themes in the Bible that celebrated God's presence in nature
and that out of these fragments we should now piece together an ecologically sound theology. That is what John
Macquarrie has suggested. He finds ripples in the Bible of an
organic rather than monarchical view of God's relation to
the creation and wants to make of these the wave of the
future.[17] Those themes are there all right, but they are far
from minor, and I do not agree that they require a view of
God as organic to, rather than monarch over the world.

The covenant of God with Noah, to take an example
previously cited, was a covenant that included the whole
created order. And the Psalms obviously delight in the
natural world, inviting us to praise the creator and to celebrate his creation. Psalm 104, to take one example, rehearses
God's initial creative act:

> Thou hast spread out the heavens like a tent
> and on their waters laid the beams of thy pavilion;
> who takest the clouds for thy chariot,
> riding on the wings of the wind;
> who makest the winds thy messengers
> and flames of fire thy servants;
> thou didst fix the earth on its foundation
> so that it can never be shaken (vv. 2–5).

This event in which the waters of chaos were separated,
making way for the mountains and the dry land, is then
linked to God's continuing care of creation:

> Thou dost make springs break out in the gullies,
>   so that their water runs between the hills.
>   The wild beasts all drink from them,
>   the wild asses quench their thirst;
>   the birds of the air nest on their banks
>   and sing songs among the leaves (vv. 10–12).

So on to praising the creator for the life that he gives to the earth, its seasons, its fruits, its creatures, and to the sea and its inhabitants.

> Bless the Lord, my soul.
> O praise the Lord (v. 35).

These are themes that are found echoed over and over again in the Psalms and throughout the Old Testament. They also find expression through to the present day in the grateful enjoyment of the fruits of the earth that is so much part of Jewish festivals, and of the weekly Sabbath eve service:

> Lord our God, King of the universe,
> we praise you whose word brings on the evening,
> whose wisdom opens heaven's gates,
> whose understanding makes times and seasons change,
> and whose will orders the stars in the arch of heaven.
> Creator of day and night, You roll light away from darkness,
> and darkness from the coming of dawn.
> Your law makes the day to pass,
> Your law brings on the night, setting day and night apart.
> You are Lord of the stars.
> O living and eternal God,
> You are our King to the end of time.
> All praise to You, O Lord, whose word makes evening fall.[18]

All this is clearly in line with the biblical witness to God as creator, and just as clearly refutes the claim that to affirm the realm of nature requires a denial of God as its monarch.

This, it seems to me, is confirmed by the place the creation stories give to man in the natural order. Whatever else is affirmed there, man is certainly set squarely in the context of the whole created order, and his history is obviously to be lived out within the framework of nature. What this means concerning his responsibility for and dominion over creation will be considered later.

(d) The fourth comment here is a brief one. If the doctrine

of creation ought to be viewed in natural as well as historical categories, the same is true of salvation and therefore of new creation. Luther was once asked what God was doing before he created the world. 'Cutting rods for the backs of fools who ask that kind of question', he is supposed to have replied. Perhaps the same fate is reserved for those who speculate on what is going to happen at the other end of time. Nevertheless, if we are to take biblical witness to the creation seriously, we have to deal with the theme of new creation and its implications not only for the history of mankind but also for the whole earth which is our home.

3. Creation and Fall

The doctrine of the fall is best understood as an attempt to give some coherent and ordered expression to an experience that is common to all of us – the conviction that things are not as they should be and that this is not the best of all possible worlds. A sense of disappointment and disillusionment with the way things are, together with an awareness that relationships are distorted and that possibilities are severely restricted, is almost universal. To make matters worse we often feel that anything we do is only likely to compound the problems. How did we get this way? Certainly the fault is not entirely ours; we can plead circumstances beyond our control. Yet we are haunted by the conviction that we are to some extent responsible and must therefore share the blame.

1. *The Experience of Alienation*

Attempts to account for this experience are as numerous as the generations, and just as varied. It has been the preoccupation of novelists as well as theologians, and playwrights and psychologists no less than historians of religion have made it a central motif. One network of explanations claims that the sense of guilt is well-founded because we have brought this trouble on ourselves, although in ways we have not understood. We may, for instance, have unwittingly angered the gods and are now suffering the consequences. That conclusion pervades primitive religions, but is not unknown in Christianity either, a fact that Albert Camus will not allow us to forget. In his novel *The Plague* he makes Father Paneloux spokesman for this view as he interprets for his congregation the horror and devastation that has struck their town of Oran:

> The first time this scourge appears in history, it was wielded to strike down the enemies of God. Pharaoh set himself up against the divine will, and the plague beat him to his knees. Thus from the dawn of recorded history the scourge of God has humbled the proud of heart and laid low those who hardened themselves against Him . . . For a long while God gazed down on this town with eyes of compassion; but He grew weary of waiting. His eternal hope was too long deferred, and now He has turned His face away from us. And so, God's light withdrawn, we walk in darkness, in the thick darkness of this plague.[1]

There are other explanations that lay the blame on ourselves but locate the cause in a different time or place. It may have been in a previous existence that we angered the gods, or became too attached to the world and its fruits so that we must now suffer the consequences. Or the blame may be laid upon previous experiences in this life but without the additional factor of divine retribution. Events in childhood, for instance, now hidden from conscious memory, may have scarred our psyche and warped our view of life, making it impossible to live in the world with freedom and enjoyment. In all of these explanations, whether primitive or sophisticated, religious, non-religious or anti-religious, there is a common theme – we are held responsible for our predicament, although in ways of which we are largely unaware.

Another set of explanations also points to a process of which we may be ignorant, but, unlike the previous ones, maintains that this is one in which we are trapped and over which we have little or no control. Our problems are due, some would claim, to the sin of our first ancestors, and people have been inheriting the consequences ever since. Our fathers have eaten sour grapes and so our teeth are set on edge. Ironically enough, some of the most outspoken critics of that sort of explanation keep close to it at this one point of laying the blame on our ancestors, for some protagonists of evolutionary theory, while repudiating what they saw as the pernicious religious myth of original sin, subscribed to a congruent myth – that our present ills derive from our animal ancestry and will remain as long as the evolutionary process is incomplete. Our fathers fought over the grapes and so we do the same.

There are many other accounts that have found wide acceptance in the past, and still do – that our feeling of alienation arises, for instance, from allowing ourselves to be tyrannized by the superstitious vestiges of a religiously sensitized conscience; or that it is inevitable so long as our true or higher self remains imprisoned in the body; or that it comes from our lack of awareness of the constellations of cosmic forces that are playing upon us and shaping our lives; or that alienation and disruption are universal human experiences because we are necessarily part of the ongoing process of history that moves by contradiction and resolution; or that a sense of alienation is unavoidable because life itself is meaningless, and any attempt to find meaning is absurd. Varied as these explanations are, they share two interesting features. The first is their tenacity. Philosophers in Greece in pre-Socratic times and in Britain in our time have proposed a naturalistic and linguistic rationale for the guilty conscience. Gnostics in the first century and theosophists in the twentieth long for the release of the soul from the bondage of the body. Babylonians centuries before Christ and devotees of astrology centuries later have looked to the stars to explain events on this planet. Heraclitus in the fourth century BC, Hegel in the nineteenth and Marxists in the twentieth explain reality in terms of flux, process, tension and conflict. Contemporary theatre of the absurd had its earlier counterpart in the drama of the Cynics.

Second, none of these explanations is merely phenomenological. None is content, in other words, to stop with a description of our predicament and its causes; all propose or imply ways of solving the problem, or at least of living with it. Discover the will of the gods and then placate them – that obviously follows from one account. From another, anticipate the release of the soul from the body by emphasizing the spiritual dimension in life; or use our reason to rid ourselves of superstitious sanctions; or affirm the absurdity of life courageously in the present. To each account of the predicament belongs an appropriate course of action.

2. *The Relation between Creation and Fall*

In proposing that we should look at the biblical themes of creation and fall I do not mean to suggest that there is one biblical view that negates all the above, a single way of accounting for the experience of alienation that has no variation or alternatives, that needs no explanation and which can be dug out of the text 'as is'. In this chapter, as in the last, no more will be attempted than to identify the theme; in later chapters the variety of approaches and of possible doctrinal and ethical conclusions will be illustrated.

In the biblical witness the problem of distortion of what is and alienation from what ought to be is a central feature. It is related to the doctrine of creation but not completely explained by it. To expand on that: our problematical situation is seen in terms of what we do, and what we do is made possible by God our creator, but there is a link in the chain of cause and effect between what we *can* do and what we *do* do that the Bible does not provide. Some other views of the world's origin and of man's place in it do supply the link and make the explanation causally complete, for instance that the event of creation is a bringing into actuality that is necessarily a fall from, or distortion of perfection, just as a building always fails to measure up to blueprint specifications. Similarly, if to create life in the world is necessarily to give the soul into captivity to the body, then one's higher or true self is unavoidably restricted by the lower or less real. If creation is seen as evolutionary process, then we inevitably suffer because caught at a stage when the process is incomplete. The biblical writers, however, see no such direct relationship between creation and fall. Man is created in such a way that he can bring this trouble upon himself, but not so that he has to.

When my two young sons wake up at daybreak yelling to each other, I appeal to my wife: 'Why do they make such a row?' Her answer: 'Because they have strong and healthy vocal chords.' That is true of course, but aggravating because it is only part of the answer. I know why they *can* yell so loudly; I wanted to know why they *do*. So with the question: 'Why have things gone wrong?' The reply, 'Because man has been created with freedom', is only half the story. It implies that our experience of alienation derives from human wrongdoing and says that we can go wrong because we are free. It does not say why we do. Yet it is just this question of why people do go wrong that the Bible leaves unanswered, not because the writers had not worked out the answer but because any such attempt destroys the terms of the question.

To put this in a slightly different way. According to the biblical accounts, it is out of human freedom that we disobey. Now to ask the question: 'What causes the disobedience?' or 'What makes us disobey?' implies a force working upon or within us that limits the scope of that freedom. That erodes responsibility and shrinks the depth-dimension of disobedience, but in the biblical witness there is no such hearing given to a plea of diminished responsibility. There is room for considering the scope of disobedience, the steps leading up to it and the conditions under which it occurs. Most commentators on the Genesis narratives do that. However, while it may be possible to identify conditions and factors involved, these should never be seen as causing the disobedience. Bonhoeffer put it this way:

In principle it is never wrong to picture to oneself the series of events preceding an evil deed. Everything however depends upon never making the series of events responsible for the deed as such; the series must go no further than the point where the chasm opens . . . the question of why evil exists is not a theological question . . . if we could answer it then *we* would not be sinners. We could make something else responsible.[2]

From this preliminary comment on the relationship between the creation of mankind and the fall we move to a closer look at each of the two terms.

3. *The Creation of Mankind*

Both the creation stories put man in the centre of the picture, although in different ways. In the first, the Priestly account, various symbolic lines converge, making man the focal point. So, for instance, the creation of everything that is leads up to the creation of man as the climax; the distinctive nature of this act is emphasized by the introduction, 'Let us make man'; only man among the creatures is made in the image of God; he is given dominion over the rest of creation; an ancient Jewish midrash comments that only after the creation of man is it said 'it was very good'. The second account says the same thing about man but in a different way. As in the first story attention is focused on man as the culmination of God's creative activity, but this time by beginning with man and then surrounding him with the rest of the creation. In this way man's unique relation to God is affirmed, yet the distinction between the two is preserved. Man is other than God, part of his creation, the dust of the ground. Into him God breathed the breath of life, making him a living being but not a divine being, and once again he is given specific responsibility. He is responsible under God to till the garden and to keep it, and to name the beasts of the field (a way of saying both to give a place to, and to put in their place), echoing the first account where man is given dominion over the rest of creation.

It is precisely this biblical view of the dominance of man that some blame for the ecological crisis. Christian apologists have argued that modern science became possible when Hebrew faith de-divinized nature, making it accessible to human manipulation without fear of tampering in an area that was taboo, and that modern technology arose out of the christian dogma of man's transcendence of and rightful mastery over nature. Add to this an implicit faith in perpetual progress which arose with the levelling out of the nature-cycle into history with a future, and all the components are there for a formula whose destructive possibilities outstrip those of the atom bomb.[3] When ascendancy over nature is interpreted as both capacity and right ruthlessly to exploit, and when all scientific-technological development is interpreted as progress, the result must be disaster.

I do not want to dispute that such a reading of the Genesis accounts could be made, nor that it may stand consciously or unconsciously behind some of what has happened.[4] If Christians want to take some credit, however remote and tenuous, for the development of science and technology, then they must also be prepared to share the blame. What I do dispute is that this is a proper reading of the biblical accounts of the creation of man. Whatever else is affirmed there, man is certainly set in the context of, and not removed from, the whole of the created order. It is certainly true that he is given a place of ascendancy, but only by a feat of desperate exegesis can this be interpreted as receiving the right ruthlessly to exploit for his own advantage. The words 'subdue' and 'have dominion' are strong,[5] but within the biblical narrative they can add up to exploitation only if God's dominion over man is similarly seen to amount to exploitation, for the Bible pictures man standing in the same relation to the rest of creation as God stands to him. In the second story it is true that man names the creatures, again symbolizing his dominion, but that reinforces his responsibility for, not his right to abuse the rest of creation. Man's participation in the whole created order is graphically portrayed here, as Bonhoeffer pointed out:

> The man whom God has created in his image . . . is the man who is formed out of earth. Darwin and Feuerbach themselves could not speak any more strongly. Man's origin is in a piece of earth. His bond with the earth belongs to his essential being.[6]

More recently Joseph Sittler has put it this way: 'The legend of creation in the first part of the Bible is presented in ecological context: God and man and the neighbor, and the whole earth as the exercise of both joy and labor.'[7] Clearly, then, the move from transcending nature to exploiting it is not warranted by the biblical witness; nor, of course, is the doctrine of inevitable progress which has sometimes been used to justify exploitation of nature. Nothing pervades the Bible more (apart from the proclamation of God's grace) than the insistence that man constantly misuses his opportunities, distorts his possibilities and precipitates his own destruction. The Judeo-christian view of history is not one of inexorable human progress, but one that looks for the opening of new possibilities by God despite human regression. But more of that later.

What I have been arguing here is not that Jews and Christians are blameless in the present crisis, but that it is a distorted or perverse interpretation of the biblical tradition that permits, much less endorses or sanctifies, human exploitation of the environment. Its roots lie not in the biblical view of man created to have dominion over nature, but in the rejection by man of God's dominion over him.

4. *The Fall*

So we are brought back to the doctrine of the fall. An inexplicable doctrine according to Pascal, yet without it we are even more inexplicable. The story of Adam and Eve has become the happy hunting-ground for generations of cartoonists and the theme of a thousand sniggers, yet without it one whole side of our being is unaccounted for. Without it our ills are wrongly diagnosed and inappropriate remedies are peddled. To take the example just referred to, we may be told that all our trouble stems from holding to a view of God as transcendent creator and of man as dominant creature. The cure? Be purged of both, is the usual prescription; back to an animistic view of God and nature, or to pantheism or panpsychism, or to God as organic to nature rather than Lord over it.

In the account of the fall in Genesis 3, however, Adam and Eve's trouble is related specifically to their disobedience. The prohibition against eating the fruit of the tree in the middle of the garden points clearly to the relationship of responsibility within which they are to live, responsible to God, and responsible for their actions in the created world. At the same time it affirms their freedom (they are able to eat the fruit although they ought not) and therefore the possibility of disobedience. Now this disobedience is seen as mounting a challenge to the authority of the creator. It begins by challenging the propriety of the prohibition: why should this limitation exist at all? They have been given authority over the whole of creation, why should this not amount to complete autonomy with no creaturely limitation? Why should God's will be the final point of reference for human action? Thus the decision to disobey becomes a usurping of God's authority. 'Knowing good and evil' refers not so much to loss of innocence as to grasping knowledge that properly belongs to God alone, to an invasion of God's realm. 'The man has become like one of us'; that was the implication to be drawn from his 'knowing good and evil'. The disobedience is therefore more than the transgression of a prohibition; it is an attempt to be like God.

All this underlines the fact that the fall, or, to use different terms, the source of our disrupted existence, or the occasion for our alienation, or the locus of our sin, occurs not at the periphery of our being but at the centre, at the very point where we are closest to God. It involves the highest aspect of our being, that which we share with God and which indeed makes us capable of becoming like God. Our predicament stems not from the fault of some lower nature but from the perversity of our best self, the image of God. This aspect of man that gives him his unique place yet leads to his downfall is often seen as his freedom. However, this does not quite fit the bill, for while his freedom is what makes disobedience possible, what constitutes his actual disobedience is his attempt to make a god of himself. Again, this disobedience is commonly described as 'turning toward the creation rather than toward the creator', but this too is only half the story. The decisive point is that man turns not only to what God has created but toward what man himself has made. So he rebels not so much by worshipping God's creation as by depending on his own capacity to create.

This view that human creativity is both the image of God and the source of alienation is seen more clearly in Genesis 11:1–9, the tower of Babel story in which the fall is projected on a community scale. Once again the people rebel by refusing to accept the place that God has given them. They want to make a name for themselves (11:4), to win their own place and guard against destruction through their own creativity, a creativity which seems to put God's own dwelling-place within their grasp. 'Come let us build ourselves a city and a tower with its top in the heavens, and make a name for ourselves; or we shall be dispersed all over the earth' (11:4). The irony of the conclusion is inescapable. In spite of their efforts, in fact precisely because of their efforts, they were scattered all over the earth and left off building the city.

Another ironical feature which the Tower and Garden stories share is that God is seen to take action to put man back in his place just when man is at the point of achieving what he is capable of, becoming like God.

> 'The man has become like one of us, knowing good and evil; what if he now reaches out his hand and takes fruit from the tree of life also, eats it and lives for ever?' So the Lord God drove him out of the garden of Eden . . . (3:22–3).
>
> Then the Lord came down to see the city and tower which mortal men had built, and he said, 'Here they are, one people with a single language, and now they have started to do this; henceforward nothing they have a mind to do will be beyond their reach. Come, let us go down there and confuse their speech, so that they will not understand what they say to one another' (11:5–7).

This raises the tantalizing question of whether we can ever be fully human and achieve our greatest potential so long as we remain dependent upon, and therefore subservient to, a creator-God. Nietzsche is only one of many who have claimed that man can come into his own only when God is dead. Others have asserted that only if God withdraws from the world and hands it over to man, or only when man realizes that there is no God and stops counting on a mythical authority-figure, will he step out of adolescence and into adulthood. Only by affirming the death of God can man be released to be himself.

This is a strong argument. It has logical force and emotional appeal, and to dismiss it as nonsense takes far too little account of its strength. What is nonsense, I think, is the attempt to square this with the biblical understanding of God, man and the world. The biblical writers consistently maintain the tension between man given his freedom yet only genuinely himself in obedience to God; man with capacity for tremendous achievement yet fully human only when this is directed by the will of God the source of creativity. Bonhoeffer too retained this tension, even if many who tried to make him a more consistent advocate of secular Christianity did not. Although it may be neater to dissolve the paradox and to say that man comes of age only when there is no God for him to depend upon, Bonhoeffer resisted that deft conclusion. In a famous passage that obstinately refuses to comply with the conclusions of the secular pietists or death-of-God theologians Bonhoeffer maintained:

> Our coming of age leads us to a true recognition of our situation before God. God would have us know that we must live as men who manage our lives without him. The God who is with us is the God who forsakes us (Mark 15:34). The God who lets us live in the world without the working hypothesis of God is the God before whom we stand continually. Before God and with God we live without God.[8]

Gregor Smith[9] was another who, while calling for a secularization of the Gospel, retained the biblical paradox by insisting that the only way people can live in a genuinely secular context is for them to reserve their ultimate allegiance for God. If not, we merely exchange one domination for another, a destructive one in place of a constructive one in Gregor Smith's opinion. Religion is replaced by one of the ideologies which promise freedom but provide bondage, which assert the priority of personal responsibility but involve people in increasingly impersonal structures, which replace historical existence with some form of collectivism. The possibility of being genuinely human disappears. The genuinely secular life, that is, being in the world and enjoying it to the full, is possible only if no aspect of this life in the world gains absolute mastery, and that depends upon reserving final loyalty for God.

This is the key theme also in H. Richard Niebuhr's *Radical Monotheism and Western Culture*.[10] Faith, according to Niebuhr, is compounded of trust and loyalty. One has trust in the object of faith that sustains life and provides meaning. In return one is loyal to that object of faith. To withhold trust and loyalty from the one sovereign God is not, however, to find freedom. A monotheistic faith is then replaced either by faith in one god whose dominion is less than absolute (e.g. state, nation, class, race) or by faith in a series of lesser gods of our own devising. In either case service to these gods leads not to freedom but to captivity, a captivity which perverts true identity by moulding it to the demands of social faith or by compressing it to the confines of lesser faiths. How can a man be truly himself when he cannot acknowledge those of other race or class or nation as his equal? How can a woman be truly herself when her worth is measured in terms of her obeisance to the gods of sexual allure or domestic efficiency?

> Nationalism shows its character as a faith whenever national welfare or survival is regarded as the supreme end of life; whenever right and wrong are made dependent on the sovereign will of the nation, however determined; whenever religion and science, education and art, are valued by the measure of their contribution to national existence . . .[11]

> The great alternative to henotheism with its relative unification of life is pluralism in faith and polytheism among the gods. Historically and in the contemporary scene such pluralism seems most frequently to follow on the dissolution of social faith. When confidence in nation or other closed society is broken, men who must live by faith take recourse to multiple centres of value and scatter their loyalties among many causes. When the half-gods go the minimal gods arrive.[12]

According to the biblical writers whose views Bonhoeffer, Gregor Smith and Niebuhr were all interpreting for their own time, to repudiate the authority of God the creator is not to fulfil the inherent possibilities in life but to bear the image of Adam which leads to death.[13] Or, to change the metaphor but not the meaning, the very structure that man builds to raise himself to the level of God and to shape his own destiny traps and crushes him. What he seeks most to avoid is exactly what happens. That is the biblical picture of man in revolt against God, bearing the image of Adam and therefore destined for death, expelled from the garden and so at odds with the whole created order, obsessed with his own capacities and scattered and divided against his fellows.

Three dimensions of this picture will now be explored a little further.

5. *Destined for Death*

(a) *As individuals.* 'As in Adam all die . . .', said St Paul. The serpent said, 'You will not die', and at first sight it seems that the serpent was right for they did not die, at least not right away, and neither do we. There is no evidence to show that sinners die younger than saints, although death comes at the end for all of us.

However, to talk about death in this context is not just to refer to the inevitable end of our physical existence, to the mortality which is part of our creatureliness. It points also to the possibility of ceasing to live while still breathing, talking, eating, drinking, and even going through the motions of making love. Our attempt to be like God is disobedience in the form of obedience, it is a will to power in the form of service, it is desire to be a creator in the form of creatureliness, it is being dead in the form of life:

A man sits in front of a bad television programme and

does not even know he is bored. He reads about enemy casualties and feels no remorse, knows about the dangers of nuclear obliteration and feels no fear. He reads about the starving millions and feels no compassion. He joins the rat-race of commerce where personal worth is measured in terms of market values and is not aware of his own anxiety. Only, his ulcers speak louder than his mind.[14]

In this way we conform to the image of Adam 'the man of dust', making our own way, valuing others not as fellow-creatures of the creator God but only as they serve our ends and contribute to our welfare, making our lives revolve around our own capacity and status. We cease to be as God intended; we begin to lose our true humanity; we begin to die. We lose not only our capacity to know God and our readiness to be near him (Adam hid from God), we also lose our ability to be genuinely with and for others (Adam blamed Eve, Eve blamed the serpent). When we are in the wrong and realize it then we lash out against others, particularly those who mean most to us.

How many crimes committed merely because their authors could not endure being wrong! I once knew a business-man who had a perfect wife, admired by all, and yet he deceived her. That man was literally enraged to be in the wrong, to be cut off from receiving, or granting himself, a certificate of virtue. The more virtues his wife displayed, the more vexed he became. Eventually, living in the wrong became unbearable to him. What do you think he did then? He gave up deceiving her? Not at all. He killed her.[15]

The man who told that story about someone else had his own first-hand experience of death this side of the grave. That is the theme of Camus's novel *The Fall*, the monologue of a highly respected citizen, widely admired for his generosity and good works. However, he finally came to see things as they really were. He had made everything revolve around his own comfort and self-esteem, and then discovered that by turning all his relationships in upon himself he was twisting and constricting them, making them wither and choking himself off from everything that made his life worthwhile:

> I have to admit it humbly, *mon cher compatriote*, I was always bursting with vanity. I, I, I is the refrain of my whole life and it could be heard in everything I said . . . When I was concerned with others, it was out of pure condescension, in utter freedom, and all the credit went to me: my self-esteem would go up a degree . . . After prolonged research on myself, I brought out the basic duplicity of the human being . . . modesty helped me to shine, humility to conquer, and virtue to oppress . . . Thus the surface of all my virtues had a less imposing reverse side . . . Despairing of love and of chastity, I at last told myself that there was nothing left but debauchery, a substitute for love, which quiets the laughter, restores silence and, above all, confers immortality. At a certain degree of lucid intoxication, lying late at night between two prostitutes and drained of all desire, hope ceases to be a torture, you see, the mind dominates the whole past, and the pain of living is for ever over.[16]

(b) *Communally.* There is another dimension to this death in the form of life. Asked why he was wearing a black armband the day after Martin Luther King was assassinated, a friend of mine answered for very many Americans, 'I'm in mourning for the whole country.' There is a sense in which this living death attacks communities, societies and nations through, and sometimes despite, individuals who comprise them.[17] We are all aware of the ways in which people can become imprisoned and dehumanized within society where individual efforts to live creatively and unselfishly seem doomed to failure.

Why have we come to this? I suggested earlier that one

major factor is the unbridled and irresponsible exercise of human creativity, creativity which observes no limits in its attempt to dominate the world, perhaps even the universe. That can now, I think, be illustrated in two or three different ways. When people set no limits, for instance, to their capacity to be 'fruitful and multiply', begetting many children in order to prove virility or fertility, or to establish a dynasty, or to secure their own future, then comes the population explosion. When productivity and the capacity to produce are taken as good in themselves without the qualifying question, 'But what is produced and for what purpose?' then the economic tide of a nation is already set. And when gross national product becomes the main criterion of a country's strength then the international economic whirlpool has already begun – markets artificially created to absorb products, pride and greed pandered to so that consumers will crave more and more, built-in obsolescence to make them want more frequently, boom-bust economies depending upon and trying to manipulate consumer spending, exhaustion of natural resources of developed nations and the plundering of the resources of others, the rich getting fewer and richer, the poor increasing and becoming poorer.

In this situation, where the emphasis is not on man's having been created but on his own creativity, human beings tend to be valued only in terms of their capacity to produce, to contribute to the economy or to add to the national achievement, and they are consequently dehumanized. They are engulfed by economic totalitarianism, or lost in political totalitarianism in which the welfare or survival of the state is the supreme end in life. Man's value, his place, indeed his very life then depends upon the state, and he is placed in a terrible dilemma. If he resists he is crushed; if he accedes then he helps to maintain the state's illusion that it is self-sustaining and the final arbiter of life. In either case his humanity is forfeit.[18]

Again, when creativity is elevated above all else, people

become obsessed with the need to extend their creative capacities. They give themselves to devising more and more complex machinery, more and more sophisticated planning, more and more technological aids to extend their power until it becomes limitless. Yet at that very point, as Moltmann observes, another kind of limit begins to emerge. Safeguards are built into machines to eliminate human error, human weakness, human interference, then human judgement and choice, and finally human freedom. Frankenstein's monster has become a reality. 'Man who rules nature via society now becomes a slave of his own products. Man's creations become autonomous, program themselves out of his control and gain the upper hand over him.'[19]

(c) *Ecological.* This reference to nature points to the third dimension of death in the form of life. Man's unbridled creativity finally threatens to become its opposite, endangering not only the individual and his society but the whole of the natural order. This is by now such a familiar theme and the evidence so overwhelming that whether we belong to the optimistic or pessimistic side in the debate, the fundamental issue is beyond dispute – that nature's capacity to sustain life as we know it is in the balance. Nature that stood in need of human ordering and caring now lies helpless before human devastation.

It also seems to me beyond dispute that this has occurred because man has not exercised his dominion over nature responsibly. His relation to the natural world has not mirrored God's relation to him. He has not exercised care, concern and restraint. In the technologically advanced areas in particular the natural world has not been given its proper place, and especially in the Protestant tradition the intrinsic value of the natural world as God's good creation has been neglected. It should by now be clear that arrogance toward nature in the name of productivity and the maximizing of profits is not just shortsightedness or carelessness or merely bad ecology; it is a profoundly sinful attitude, amounting to an attack against the neighbour (present and future) and against the natural world, and so against God who is creator of both.

The fallenness of human existence therefore extends beyond the levels of individual ethics and of political power and international conflict to the place of humanity within, and the future of, the whole of the created order. In the early Church a doctrine which divided soul and body and looked for salvation only for the soul was condemned as 'blasphemy of the creation'. Recently a rabbi in Chicago used the same term for the pollution of Lake Michigan, and it seems to me that he was right, for we blaspheme as much by deed as by doctrine, and by attacking nature as well as attacking man.

If this broader perspective is to be brought to bear on understanding our fallen existence it must also inform our hope for new creation, a hope which must therefore not be restricted to the individual, nor to the household of faith, nor even to the community of humankind, but must somehow include hope for the whole of the created order.

4. Creation and New Creation

'As it was in the beginning, is now and ever shall be, world
without end, Amen.' In this familiar ascription of glory,
what does the 'it' refer to? Is it the world that was and is
and ever shall be? If so then the Puritans had some justification for banning this 'lesser doxology' as unscriptural. Or
does the 'it' refer to 'the Father, Son and Holy Spirit'? We
do speak of God as the same yesterday, today and for ever,
although I am not convinced that we should, for that owes
more to a philosophical notion of a realm of eternal perfection above human history than to the biblical God who is
involved with history, and in any case 'it' is hardly an
appropriate pronoun for the Holy Trinity! 'Glory be to the
Father . . .' is the way the doxology begins, and most likely
it is the glory due to God that is from the beginning and to
eternity. But does it really matter so long as we assert
that the basis for our faith and hope, and therefore for our
songs of praise, is an unchangeable core at the centre of
things?

1. Faith, Hope and Change

Jürgen Moltmann is right when he claims that it matters a
great deal because it is just this holding to the unchangeable
that has left the Church with virtually nothing else to offer
the world. He maintains that when Christians became
anxious about the future they searched in faith for the
stability of eternity to stave off the terrors of time. In the last
century such 'faith without hope' within the Church finally
drew a reaction of 'hope without faith' from outside. Now
the barriers are up, as he puts it, between Christians who

look to the eternal and unchanging while unbelievers look to the future and hope for change.[1]

This is just the reverse of the situation in which Israel found herself. There, as we have seen, the followers of Yahweh took exactly the opposite course, at odds with their neighbours who were trying to find their place in the cycle of nature and who, unable to fathom the meaning of history and to face its terrors, looked for security in the eternal renewal of the seasons and the courses of the stars. The people of Israel, on the other hand, were called to put their faith in God who came to them within history so that purpose and meaning were to be found by facing historical events rather than escaping them. They did not always heed the call, as the biblical narratives make clear. The attraction of the nature-gods persisted because they offered stability and security. That was alluring to those who were suffering in the present turmoil and could find no assurance of relief in history. Paradoxically it was also attractive to those at the other end of the scale, those who were very comfortable and well satisfied with their situation. The wealthy and powerful were certainly not looking for radical change and so they welcomed the worship of gods who took no interest in anything so crassly historical as social justice. It is therefore no coincidence that the prophetic denunciation of the Baalim goes along with condemnation of those who grind the face of the poor and sell them for a pair of shoes. The prophets spoke for a God who, far from guaranteeing continuity of things as they were, promised their end, a tearing down to the foundations before the rebuilding of a new order.

To affirm God as creator, therefore, was to affirm his creative presence primarily in the history of the people, at the same time calling them to put their faith in God who gives meaning and purpose to that history, and to order their lives so that they observed the terms of the covenant God had made with them. Consequently the transformation of the nature-myths and festivals that we have already referred to was not done in order to provide history with the same quality of unchanging stability and rhythm that belonged to nature. It was to affirm that change and movement were what made history what it was, the ground on which the creator-God had chosen to meet his people. Change was therefore not to be feared, decried or avoided. Its meaning was to be sought, and the participation of the people directed, by referring to the terms of the covenant which constituted them a people in the first place.

One implication of this flattening out of the cycle of nature into the vector of history was that history which had a beginning was also to have an end. The starting-point for Israel's faith was her present experience of God in history, and from that there were projections in two directions, one back to the beginning of history and one forward to the consummation. The creation at the beginning we looked at in chapter 2; we now turn to new creation expected at the end.

2. *The Old Testament and New Creation*

In the Old Testament the power of God to create anew belonged to the present experience of the people. Yahweh is the one who now saves and renews his people Israel according to the covenant, and this saving and renewing is often depicted as an act of new creation. In Psalm 19, for example, it is God the creator of the universe whose glory is told out by the heavens and who has made a covenant with his people, giving them the law, who now cleanses and saves his people. Psalm 95 calls for praise of God who is the creator of all things, who also created Israel and upon whose creative power her present salvation depends. Psalm 18, a psalm of deliverance and redemption, relies heavily upon the imagery of creation in which the waters of chaos are overcome and light is brought out of darkness:

When the bonds of death held me fast,
destructive torrents overtook me,
the bonds of Sheol tightened round me,
the snares of death were set to catch me;
then in anguish of heart I cried to the Lord,
I called for help to my God;
he heard me from his temple,
and my cry reached his ears.
The earth heaved and quaked,
the foundations of the mountains shook;
they heaved, because he was angry . . .
He reached down from the height and took me,
he drew me out of mighty waters,
he rescued me from my enemies, strong as they were,
from my foes when they grew too powerful for me
(vv. 4–7, 16–17).

This imagery of the saving activity of God as new creation in the present, manifesting the same power that brought the earth and the nation into being in the first place, is seen throughout the Old Testament, as John Reumann has recently illustrated.[2]

Many other passages refer to this same creative and redeeming power of God but look for it more especially in the future. Psalm 77, for example, begins with a despairing cry about present trouble and a bleak future, but then goes on to recall God's creative power that parted the waters of chaos at the beginning and at the Red Sea, and longs for this to occur again. The lament of Psalm 74 also calls upon God to rise up and maintain his cause, to 'restore what was ruined beyond repair', God who divided the sea by his might, crushed the sea-monster, who opened the way for spring and torrent and gave the dry land, who ordained the light of the moon and sun, the seasons of summer and winter and who has fixed all the regions of the earth.

Some of the most explicit expressions of hope couched in

terms of new creation are found in second Isaiah. Recalling
the myth of creation the prophet summons God to act as in
days of old when he divided the waters at the exodus as he
had parted the waters of chaos, creating his people as he had
created the earth. So the time will come when his people will
again pass through the chaotic waters to the land of promise:

> Awake, awake, put on your strength, O arm of the Lord,
>   awake as you did long ago, in days gone by.
>   Was it not you
> who hacked the Rahab in pieces and ran the dragon through?
>   Was it not you
> who dried up the sea, the waters of the great abyss,
> and made the ocean depths a path for the ransomed?
>   So the Lord's people shall come back, set free,
>   and enter Zion with shouts of triumph,
>   crowned with everlasting joy;
>   joy and gladness shall overtake them as they come,
>   and sorrow and sighing shall flee away (Isa. 51:9–11).

Citing this passage and others in Isaiah in which Israel's
hope for the consummation is portrayed in terms of the new
creation, Bernhard Anderson comments:

> We stand here on the threshold of the understanding that
> creation has an eschatological dimension. Men may put
> their trust in life's meaning in spite of the chaotic threats
> of history because the whole historical drama from be-
> ginning to end is enfolded in the purpose of God who is
> worshipped as creator and redeemer.[3]

But where does this leave us? No doubt the cycle of
nature as source of security has been abandoned, but has the
move to history done anything to open up the future? Are
we not now caught in another cycle, the cycle of history in
which nothing really new happens either, in which the
present is an echo of the past and the future a return to the
beginning?

It is certainly true that what is expected in the future is described in terms of what has been known in the past, but at least from the time of the major prophets this was to be no mere repetition of the past. It was to be significantly new. New in the *first* place because Israel must now look forward to judgement and destruction such as she has never known before. No dependence upon her past history will save her, no clinging to past institutions such as Jerusalem nor to past shibboleths as 'the Temple of the Lord, the Temple of the Lord' will provide immunity, because out of that same past comes the reason for judgement. Past actions that break the covenant are the ground for Israel's judgement, but nothing in the past can prepare her for the kind of judgement that is coming. Amos warns his hearers of its magnitude by reminding them of the awesome power of God. He 'who builds his stair up to the heavens and arches his ceiling over the earth' will also touch the earth so that it melts and 'all who dwell on it mourn' (9:5–6). Similarly Jeremiah warns that the impending destruction will be like nothing so far known, to be compared only with what no human has witnessed, the chaos before the world began:

> I saw the earth, and it was without form and void;[4]
>> the heavens, and their light was gone . . .
> I saw, and there was no man,
>> and the very birds had taken flight (4:23,25).

But this will not simply be a return to nothing and so the end of everything, for although 'the whole land shall be desolate', says the Lord, 'I will not make an end of it' (4:28).

Therefore what was expected will be new in the *second* place because beyond the destruction which will effect a radical break with the past there will be a new action of God, not on the basis of the old covenant for that is over and done with, but arising out of a new relationship between God and his people. With this, says Moltmann, 'the basis of salvation for Israel shifts from the past into the future. Israel's faith

changes from a living memory into a living hope.'[5] Nevertheless, while this faith may now look to the future instead of
the past, what is expected can only be described, as Moltmann himself acknowledges, by analogy with the past, out
of the memory of God's faithfulness. Hosea, for example,
looks for a new occupation of the land, Amos the reinstatement of the family of Jacob, Ezekiel a new temple in a new
city, Isaiah a new David, second Isaiah a new exodus, and
Jeremiah a new covenant. But while the analogy with the
past is clearly evident, so is the dimension of the radically
new. In Jeremiah, for example, it is obvious that the new
creation of the people was not to be simply another name for
the redeeming activity of God assured under the old covenant, and that this is to be a genuinely new creation is confirmed by the familiar blending of images of primeval chaos
and the exodus by which it is described. This is not a return
to past events of creation but will be, as they were, the
occasion for ushering in the radically new (Jer. 31:31–5).
In second Isaiah there is a similar emphasis on the expectation of a new beginning, and the same image is used:

> Thus says the Lord,
> who opened a way in the sea
> and a path through mighty waters . . .
> Cease to dwell on days gone by
> and to brood over past history.
> Here and now I will do a new thing;
>   this moment it will break from the bud
>
> (43:16,19).

So Israel is not to live in the past but to hope for the
future, and this is depicted as renewal not simply of the
people but of the whole creation. That is the *third* sense in
which new creation is to be significantly new – the promise
of God on which his people depend is seen to include all
people, in fact the whole inhabited earth and the realm of
nature.[6] There are passages in the book of Isaiah from all the

prophetic strands which give shape and colour to this expectation. The wolf will live with the sheep and the leopard lie down with the kid (11:6).[7] There will be paths in the desert and water in the wilderness (43:19,20), pine trees in place of camel-thorn and myrtles instead of briars (55:12–13). In these verses God's transforming power in nature remains tied to his redemption of Israel, for the signs of renewal in nature provide little more than the setting for the salvation of the people. It is for Israel that there will be a path in the desert and water in the wilderness, for Israel that 'mountains and hills shall break into cries of joy, and all the trees of the wild shall clap their hands'. In chapter 66, however, the transformation is more far-reaching, encompassing all nations and the whole of nature in the event of new creation:

> . . . behold, I create
> new heavens and a new earth.
>> Former things shall no more be remembered
>> nor shall they be called to mind.
>> Rejoice and be filled with delight,
>> you boundless realms which I create (65:17–18).

> Then I myself will come to gather all nations and races,
>> and they shall come and see my glory;
>> and I will perform a sign among them . . .
> For, as the new heavens and the new earth
> which I am making shall endure in my sight,
>> says the Lord,
> so shall your race and your name endure;
>> and month by month at the new moon,
>> week by week on the sabbath,
> all mankind shall come to bow down before me,
>> says the Lord (66:18, 22–3).

These last verses are, of course, apocalyptic, and it seems that their universal scope was already an embarrassment to the interpolator (vv. 20, 22, 24) who wanted to narrow the range of God's redemptive purpose once more. They are also regarded as something of an aberration these days, especially by those who advocate salvation-history as *the* key to interpreting the biblical witness, because they stubbornly retain elements of nature-mythology that are not reducible to *Heilsgeschichte*. Some openly scorn them because taken to dissipate proper concern for the present by concentrating on fanciful speculation about the future.

What these last two estimates fail to recognize, however, is that apocalyptic supplies a dimension without which salvation-history becomes shallow, and social reform amounts to an exercise in futility and despair. To take salvation-history first, without belief in a God who is able to act in a way that past history gives us no right to expect, the history of salvation becomes just as repetitive and predictable as the cycle of nature. There can be nothing new because everything must have its historical precedent, and God is then bound within history as the nature-gods were tied to the cycle of the seasons. The apocalyptic vision restores God's absoluteness and gives newness to history by going outside the process of history for its images, portraying God's future actions as comparable only to the first creation before the dawn of history, unprecedented in kind and cosmic in scope. Similarly with social action, it becomes pointless without this apocalyptic vision because there are no grounds in past history for expecting a lasting change for the better in human affairs. Only belief in God as one who breaks in against the possibilities resident within human history can provide the hope that makes any present reforming action worth the effort. Far from destroying the basis for social concern, the apocalyptic vision provides one that could hardly be more relevant to the present situation of crisis compounding crisis, portraying as it does a God who brings new possibilities out of what historical judgement calls impossibilities.

3. *The new testament*

(a) *Jesus Christ and the new creation.* In the New Testament witness to Jesus Christ, the sense of the new is like ink on the pages, giving shape and substance to everything that is said. The coming of the Lord is itself an act of new creation by the Spirit and will mean a new outpouring of Spirit on all flesh. His coming means new hope for the humble and the hungry, a new deliverance for captives. His words and actions are so unprecedented that people are dumbfounded at the 'new teaching'; never before have they known the like. He gives new sight to the blind, new strength to wasted limbs, new direction to twisted lives, new life to the dead. He is the mediator of a new covenant, and those who hear and respond become a new people, a new creation. They are given a new name, speak a new tongue, receive a new commission and are under a new command to love as they have been loved. They see signs of a new age and are themselves part of that age; they look for its fulfilment in a new heaven and a new earth, for their Lord makes all things new.

All this, of course, is directly related to Jesus Christ, for in his life and death and resurrection the power of God to create anew is already known. This relation between Jesus Christ and the new creation the New Testament writers portray in different ways. Some of the Synoptic narratives, for example, provide the readers with clues, some more obvious than others, from which to draw their own conclusions. That is the intention of Mark's account of the stilling of the storm,[8] which comes to its climax with the question, 'Who can this be? Even the wind and the sea obey him.' Who indeed? Who else addressed the sea and brought order out of watery chaos? The same conclusion is invited by the Markan account of Jesus' walking on the sea. When he got into the boat with his disciples the wind dropped, and Mark concluded: 'At this they were completely dumbfounded, for they had not understood the incident of the loaves; their minds were closed.'[9] But why would an understanding of the loaves have made them less astonished at Jesus' power over the wind and waves? Yahweh was known as the creator and sustainer of his people, making them a people by bringing them through the waters of exodus, feeding them manna in the desert. Now Jesus too had fed the people in the wilderness. If the disciples had understood the full significance of *that* (as the reader is now being invited by Mark to do) they would have seen him sharing the power of God to sustain. They would not then have been so astonished that he shared the power of God over the wind and waves.[10]

In one of the New Testament courses taught by Howard Kee I remember his making the same point about the exorcism narratives in Mark.[11] In these accounts Jesus is said to have rebuked (*epitiman*) the evil spirit, and this is the same word as that used in the stilling of the storm where he rebuked the elements. Qumran texts show that the Semitic equivalent is a term sometimes used in the Old Testament to describe God's command to the chaotic waters (Pss. 18:16; 104:7). So, Kee has suggested, Jesus' healing by exorcism is seen by Mark to be more than expulsion of a demon, more even than the beginning of the end for the prince of demons, although it is that. It confirms the beginning of that new age in which all the powers of darkness and evil are subjugated by the power of new creation in Jesus Christ.

The decisive role of Jesus Christ in this event of new creation is made more explicit elsewhere.[12] Certainly the prologue to the fourth Gospel superimposes the picture of Christ's coming upon that of the first creation, making sure that the reader sees each in the light of the other. The accounts of the last supper also make it clear that in Christ the new covenant is being established as Jeremiah had foretold. Paul too used the images of creation and new creation to convey the significance of Christ and to describe what happens in the lives of those who respond. 'For the same God who said, "Out of darkness let light shine", has caused his light to shine within us, to give the light of revelation – the revelation of the glory of God in the face of Jesus Christ' (2 Cor. 4:6). Christ is the new Adam, a life-giving spirit through whom we are made into a new image, his image. That is an act of new creation, for when anyone is united to Christ the new order has already begun (2 Cor. 15:17).

Paul shows also that this new creation which Christ effects in human life is somehow involved with the whole created order. Nature which has also suffered the ravages of the fall is to know release and to enjoy the benefits of new creation (Rom. 8:12 ff.). In Colossians the victory of Christ on the cross is made to reflect his primacy over the whole created order. It is in fact a reassertion of the creative role which was his from the beginning (Col. 1:17–18).[13]

Just as the apocalyptic literature of the Old Testament broadened the scope of the expected new creation to include all people and all creatures, so in the New Testament the book of Revelation more graphically than any other conveys the good news of salvation in Christ in terms of new creation. A new name is to be given (2:17), a new song will be sung (5:9; 14:3), the new Jerusalem will be established (3:12; 21:2), there will in fact be a new heaven and a new earth (21:1). The Lamb who sits on the throne will make all things new (21:5). In these descriptions of what is to come 'almost every sentence is related to creation and corresponds to something in the primal history, Genesis 1–11 . . . The end time is described as creation made whole again.'[14] The boundaries of both judgement and salvation are pushed beyond the nation Israel to include all peoples. The pictures of the new era included the whole of the natural order.

(b) *The extent of new creation.* All this leaves us with a great many questions. If Jesus did manifest God's power of new creation, what was really new? What changed with his coming? What has yet to be fulfilled? Some people at the time apparently were struck with the newness of his life and teaching. Some experienced something new in themselves, new power and new direction. Some saw other people and the whole world in a new light; former differences ceased to count. Those who believed in Christ witnessed to the resurrection, life out of death, a new act of creation out of nothing, the end of one history and the beginning of a new.

But what did this amount to? If this was new creation, what had happened to the world? What difference had been made in the life of nations and i.. the whole created order? The answer to that, at least within the lifetime of the first witnesses, was 'precious little', and we may be inclined to say the same. If we now live in the era of new creation, what must chaos have been like?

Why are there so few signs of the new creation in the world at large? We have no monopoly on attempts to answer that question. Some have said that new creation is here all right, but that since it is heir to the Jewish prophetic tradition it is not all that new. Others have said that it is here but operating only at the level of personal experience of the individual or of the spiritual experience and liturgy of the faith-community, but not at the more visible levels of society or nature. Again, some have maintained that it is radically new and does involve the whole of history and the natural world, but has yet to be fulfilled. We therefore live in the time between the first signs of new creation in Christ and its fulfilment at the end of the age. That became the normative view in the early Church. Paul certainly longed for the fulfilment that had yet to come, but this was not the only view, and, even if it did become the normative one, what are we to make of it today? To elaborate on these two points:

(i) Ernst Käsemann in particular has identified various early answers to the question 'How new was the new?' and it is interesting to follow Moltmann's account of how the early christian communities were shaped by their answer to that question.[15] For example, the earliest Jewish-christian community that gathered around Peter and Jerusalem apparently saw the risen one as Son of David, the Messiah of Israel. Consequently it saw itself in continuity with Israel as the reconstituted twelve tribes under twelve apostles, needing to maintain the numerical parallel by lot, upholding the law and the rite of circumcision, and with no impetus toward mission to the Gentiles. Another community, the one to which Stephen belonged, must have taken a more radical view of what had happened in Christ. Its members acknowledged his continuity with the prophets of Israel, but then emphasized the condemnation and rejection that these prophets suffered at the hands of the Jewish establishment. So they maintained that the coming of Jesus represented a break with and judgement upon the Judaism that centred on priesthood, temple and synagogue. Persecuted for what was seen as blasphemous interpretation of God's dealing with his people, they fled to Antioch where they saw Gentiles, without first becoming Jews, receiving the Spirit of the Lord. Under the impact of this experience and their interpretation of it a new community grew in which the former differences, while still present, had no force as distinctions. Christians at Corinth apparently went even further, not only seeing themselves as the new people of God but believing that they were already living in the fulness of God's new era. They equated freedom in this new creation with liberation from all restrictions on the body, and from all obligations to law and society. Already living in the final age with nothing new to hope for, they were liberated to revel in everything in the here and now.

Where does Paul fit into this scheme? At first sight, somewhere between Corinth and Jerusalem, affirming the universal scope of the Gospel against Jerusalem, yet preserving the Old Testament heritage against Corinth; denouncing those who wanted to re-impose the Law on the newly baptized, yet equally critical of those who saw no obligation placed upon them by the terms of the Gospel. It soon becomes clear, however, that it is a mistake to locate Paul in the middle of the road to anywhere. He was, in fact, more radical than the Corinthians because he was not prepared, as they were, to settle for a new creation restricted to individual and spiritual dimensions. It had to be seen to encompass the whole of life, the life of people and of nations, the whole realm of nature. The totally new situation brought about by Jesus' resurrection had no human parallel; it could be described only in terms of the creative power of God who calls into being that which was not. Of course if new creation is to have these dimensions then it cannot yet be here, at least not in its fulness, and that was Paul's conclusion. New creation is here in the resurrection of Christ and we are raised to new life in him; but we are not yet raised to the new life beyond the grave. Those in Christ are a new creation, yet the whole creation still suffers in bondage, waiting for the day of its release.

(ii) It is hardly necessary to point out that these different views about new creation were far from theoretical speculation, irrelevant to the daily life of Christians in the world. They had, as I have briefly indicated, profound impact upon the way those early Christians saw their ethical responsibilities as individuals and as communities called to witness to the Gospel in a largely alien world. It is therefore not forcing this New Testament witness out of context to press the question: what conclusions should *now* be drawn by a community which has that view of new creation, new creation present in Christ but still to be fulfilled not only in the individual and spiritual dimension but within the whole creation?

The answer to that cannot be read off some exegetical teleprinter that transmits in plain type from the first century to the twentieth. It depends to a considerable extent on the way one brings to bear conclusions about the other two themes we have been discussing, namely, God the creator and the fallen creation.

For example, one view taken of God the creator creating out of nothing concludes that he will again create out of nothing that man does. All that the faith-community can do is to await his intervention at the end of time. Another is that God, having handed over responsibility for the world to man, now exercises creative power only through him ('He has no hands but our hands . . .'). Consequently the fulfilment of new creation awaits responsible human initiative. Another maintains that although the human race was given authority over the rest of creation by God, it is now so fallen and has so distorted the world that only an act of God that runs counter to human capacity and expectation will achieve the new creation. Therefore the role of the community of faith is to be critical, iconoclastic, de-idolizing human achievements, affirming that none can be identified as God's work of new creation. Yet another, beginning with the affirmation that Jesus Christ was God's new creation, concludes that the Church as the body of Christ should now embody Christ's life in her own, anticipating the new creation by being oriented toward the poor and weak and homeless, giving her life for the unrighteous and the ungodly, living out the signs of new creation in the sight of the wider community.

From these brief comments we can see that to believe in Jesus Christ as God's new creation and to anticipate the fulfilment of that new creation clearly has implications for the life of the Church, but just as clearly it is no simple matter to decide what these implications are. Conclusions are shaped to a great extent by prior conclusions about the relation between God and his creation, and between man and the world. The same can be said about looking for the renewal of the whole created order. Those who take seriously the biblical testimony about this still draw very different conclusions about how we should take it, as we can see by looking again at two segments of the New Testament witness. Whatever else is obscure in the imagery of the book of Revelation, it is clear that this new creation is not just a return to Paradise Lost. It is easy to be overawed by the scholarly tag-phrase *Urzeit gleich Endzeit*[16] and so to miss the significance of suggestions in the biblical text itself that the end is to be more than the beginning. The descriptions certainly draw on the imagery of the beginning, but just as certainly omega is to be more than alpha, as Moltmann has observed.[17] On that day not only will there be light out of darkness but darkness will be overcome; there will be no more night. The waters of chaos are not just separated, they disappear; no longer will there be any threatening sea. God will come, not just to walk with man in the garden but to make his dwelling-place with him. Paul also set the new creation in cosmic perspective:

> The created universe waits with eager expectation for God's sons to be revealed. It was made the victim of frustration, not by its own choice, but because of him who made it so; yet always there was hope, because the universe itself is to be freed from the shackles of mortality and enter upon the liberty and splendour of the children of God . . . (Rom. 8:19–21).

What are we to make of this involvement of the whole 'created universe' in the new creation? It would be tempting to disregard it as fanciful embroidery, a distracting embellishment to the New Testament not integral to its message and not vital to the life of the people. There is, however, too much evidence to the contrary. It was not peripheral, and, as we have seen, what was thought about the scope of new creation was directly related to how early Christians lived out the Gospel. It is true that some scholars do reject this witness to cosmic re-creation simply on the grounds of its apocalyptic form. Bultmann, for example,[18] is inclined to see all such writing as out of harmony with the existential eschatology of Paul and John, even when such passages are acknowledged to be Pauline. But Schweitzer, Käsemann and Wilder are only three among many who have demonstrated the centrality of apocalyptic which cannot be excluded without destroying the heart of the Gospel. Therefore unless we are to think about new creation in isolation from the biblical witness or in the presence of only an arbitrarily censored version we cannot simply overlook this cosmic dimension. We have somehow to come to terms with it.

It is not difficult to see how the biblical writers were able to fit it into their scheme. It was consistent with their belief in God as creator, and with the way in which that belief developed. When the experience of God in the history of the people was projected back to the beginning it included God as the creator of all that is, creator of nature as well as of history. It therefore completed the pattern to project forward to the end, seeing him re-creating all that is, nature as well as history.[19] However, it is one thing to appreciate the literary ingenuity of the biblical authors; it is another to recognize their meaning and to take it seriously for ourselves. Theologians who agree on the importance of the theme of the renewal of the whole of creation are far from agreement on what we should make of it.

Karl Barth, for example, suggests that the emphasis should be not on man plus the rest of the natural world waiting for re-creation, but on those who know the first-fruits of the Spirit longing for the time when all will know the redemption of mankind. Emil Brunner, on the other hand, read this in the context of his understanding of the 'orders of creation', of family or state, for example, now distorted because of man's sin, partly restored in the present through faith, finally to be restored at the end-time. Rudolf Bultmann maintains that it is man's relation to the creation and not the world of nature itself that is distorted because man has placed himself under the domination of the world. It is therefore this relationship to the world that is to be renewed. Joseph Sittler is more explicit than that, claiming that nature which once threatened man is now so much at his mercy that she lies suppliant before him, living by his sufferance and dying under his attack. So creation waits for men of faith to be what they are called to be – sons of God who replenish rather than ravish the rest of creation. C. F. D. Moule makes the same point,[20] that man's sonship, when it becomes what it should be, will set nature free from the decay that results from human greed, enabling it once again to be used according to God's purpose. John Reumann, however, objects that these views fail to recognize that the biblical witness always gives precedence to the theme of redemption and that therefore Romans 8 must be read as referring to 'the new creaturehood of Christian believers, not a cosmic daydream'.[21]

Obviously these variations reflect more than a disagreement over translation, context or 'insight into the biblical mind'. They point to differences in theological perspective from which the texts are viewed and indeed from which all three themes of creation, fall and new creation are approached. The rest of this book will be given to considering in more detail what happens when these inter-related themes are approached from different theological viewpoints, and what conclusions can then be drawn about living faithfully in the created world.

B. THEOLOGICAL PERSPECTIVES

5. Transcendentalist: Karl Barth

At the end of the discussion on new creation it was becoming obvious that conclusions drawn about this and about the themes of creation and fall will vary with the kind of questions put, with the presuppositions behind the questions, and with the frame of reference that shapes both questions and answers. In this and succeeding chapters four kinds of approach will be described in order to compare the varying conclusions that are reached. Each of the approaches has been given a label, and in each case the spotlight falls on one theologian although others do make an appearance.

This way of proceeding has its problems. No label is entirely appropriate. No theologian settles comfortably into a mould prepared for him by someone else. No type-casting of approaches can retain the range of subtleties and shadings that the works of the theologians display. Consequently any grouping of outlooks is to some extent limited because no one ever conforms completely to type. Nevertheless to reproduce the ideas of theologians without attempting to classify them is just as limiting, and to construct model approaches without relating them to actual exponents is even more artificial. In any case this problem of method is not confined to theology, and when it occurs in other fields it does not lead to cancellation because the programme is thought to be too important for that. In politics, for instance, it was obviously important to know what the attitude of the various parties was toward the EEC. It could be argued that the labels 'Conservative', 'Labour' and 'Liberal' did not accurately reflect the policies of the parties on that issue, but they were still useful for purposes of identification. It is true that there were differences of opinion within the parties, and that on this issue some members of parliament may have had views more in keeping with those of other parties than their own, but that shows the value of linking particular people with typical approaches. For the sake of clarity and of contrast the views of the leaders were taken as representative (as on most political themes) and expounded as such. In the same way here, the limitations of labels and of identifying particular people with general approaches are recognized, but the method is followed in order to provide content and contrast, and to sharpen discussion of the issues involved.

1. *Starting-point : The Radical Otherness of God*

The transcendentalist approach is most readily identified, at least in this century, with the theology of Karl Barth, more accurately perhaps, as he himself points out, with Barth of the nineteen-twenties. He comments on this approach in retrospect:

> The stone wall we first ran up against was that the theme of the Bible is the deity of God, more exactly God's deity – God's independence and particular character, not only in relation to the natural but also to the spiritual cosmos, God's absolutely unique existence, might and initiative, above all in relation to man. Only in this manner were we able to understand the voice of the Old and New Testaments. Only with this perspective did we feel we could henceforth be theologians and, in particular, preachers, ministers of the divine word.[1]

That was the way Barth and others associated with him in *crisis theology* saw things at the time. The situation had developed because in the previous century Protestant orthodoxy came under sustained attack, especially from scientific humanism, and the theological defences built to fend off the attack were now crumbling. The attack had hit hard at the foundations on which belief had traditionally been built – the authority of scripture, the certainty of the existence of God, the divinity of Christ and the philosophically impregnable theological systems. When the scientific method of inquiry was rigorously applied the Bible, for example, lost its untouchable infallible status, God's existence became a matter for empirical investigation, Jesus' divinity was open to historical inquiry, and theological systems were judged by their appeal to human experience. Response varied from reactionary conservatism to convinced atheism, from those who denied any validity to the scientific method, protecting their belief by embalming it, to those who came to worship science, putting it in place of God. One influential group, however, the Liberals, set out to meet the challenge on the challengers' own ground maintaining that by beginning with empirically verifiable history (the Jesus of the past divested of mythological trappings, or the experience of everyman in present history) it was possible to build up a new inductive theological system and thus to re-establish the faith. Not only were the methods of science seen to be consistent with those of theology but its achievements were understood to reinforce faith. The increasing control of the natural world which technology made possible was, for instance, seen as a sign of the developing kingdom of God on earth.

By the end of the First World War this approach had come under increasingly heavy fire, and Barth records the factors which led him finally to make the break: the 're-ligionistic, anthropocentric and in this sense humanistic' tendencies of evangelical theology, the encounter with socialism 'which opened our eyes to the fact that God might be actually wholly other than the God confined to the musty shell of the Christian-religious self-consciousness', the 'suddenly darkened outlook for the world' which gave the lie to optimistic estimates of human achievements, 'or was it something

more fundamental than all that, namely the discovery that
the theme of the Bible, contrary to the orthodox exegesis
which we inherited, certainly could not be man's religion
and religious morality and certainly not his own secret
divinity?'[2]

Liberalism was therefore seen to be vulnerable at many
points and Barth spearheaded the theological attack. He
came to believe that liberal theology led only to a new
Babylonian captivity. If there is a God at all worthy of the
name, Barth argued, one who calls forth our obedience and
loyalty and worship, then he must be the creator-redeemer
who really meets the genuine need of humanity. He cannot
then be a mere extension of human thoughts and capacities,
for to begin with human experience and to build up a
knowledge of God from there is to build a tower of Babel
theology which does not reach God at all, but only leaves
man with his head in the clouds. When the Church begins
with human experience it is left with nothing worthwhile to
say and nothing to do except to cover up the silence with the
noise of busyness. What is needed is a Bethel theology that
witnesses to a God who takes initiative and comes to man
'vertically down from above', a theology therefore that begins
with God and his word, with what he does for man and says
to man.

What happens when our three themes are approached
from this perspective?

2. *God the Creator*

The statement: 'God is the Creator of the World' has in
the main a double content: it speaks of the *freedom* of
God (one could also say: of His *holiness*) over against the
world, and of His *relationship* (one could also say: of His
love) to the world.[3]

(a) Taking first the aspect of God's freedom over against the world, to affirm that God is creator is to emphasize God's 'absolutely unique existence',[4] the 'infinite qualitative distinction' between God and man. It is another way of depicting God as 'wholly other' and of stressing the distinction between God who has created everything and everything that has been created. It is to deny those views of the God-world relation that assert a continuity between them, for instance that the world is somehow spun out of the being of God, or that the world is an extension of God, or is God in the process of development.[5] It is therefore to define the creator-creature structure within which we all live and which must serve as the framework for understanding and talking about God, man and the world. This is an asymmetric structure, and unless that is recognized doctrinal statements may seem to make some sense but are in fact nonsense. Small boy to father: 'I want to marry Grandma.' Father replies: 'You can't; it's just not done.' Small boy: 'Why not? You married my mother, why can't I marry yours?' Full marks to the small boy's intuitive grasp of the principle of reciprocity, and sooner or later he will find out that it has to be fitted into a wider structure of both life and language. In the same way any doctrinal statement, however cogent it may on the surface appear to be, must be set within the framework provided by belief in God as creator if it is to make any real sense.

It is within this context, for instance, that we are to understand the traditional view of the hiddenness of God. Pascal maintained that a religion which does not say that God is hidden is not true. That may seem to put the theologian at an impossible disadvantage, but in a way it is a matter of common sense. We do not expect to find God by looking around for him, and to know that he is not continuous with his creation saves us from searching for him in the wrong places, and from falling into idolatry by identifying people, things or institutions as God. To assert God's 'freedom over against the world' also enables us to live in the world and to make use of what nature offers, free from the superstitious fear that we are interfering with the divine and thus courting retribution.[6] Pascal went on to say, however, that a religion that does not say why God is hidden is not instructive.[7] According to the transcendentalist view, God is hidden because he is God and we are not. It is not that our eyes are too dim to penetrate far enough into the distance or too distracted to look in the right direction. God's hiddenness is not a reflection of our infirmity; it belongs to him as God, *ex officio* as it were.

Similarly the holiness of God is to be understood within the same set of theological co-ordinates, the creator-creature structure. It makes theological nonsense to construct some pattern of moral conduct from human experience of living in the world, to see that God fits into that pattern or even exemplifies it perfectly, and then to conclude: 'God is therefore holy.' It is the holiness of God which conveys to us the overwhelming sense of his otherness to which we can respond only in awe that both fascinates us and overcomes us,[8] so that we are in a way content that God should remain hidden. It was out of kindness that God veiled the glory of his face from the people.

A further implication of this way of looking at the creator-creature structure is that we can have no knowledge of God, not even that he is our creator, until he chooses to make himself known. This he has not done in nature, at least not in a way that leads directly from observation to the conclusion that there is a creator, for there is a discontinuity between creation and its creator. Nor are we able to argue from aspects of our own being to features of the being of God, for there is no analogy of being between creator and creature. Knowledge of God can come only as he chooses to break through the structural barrier, to bridge the creator-creature gulf, to come out of hiding and to reveal himself to us.

This, Barth maintains, God has done in the decisive event of Jesus Christ. He has taken the initiative, bridging the gulf in the one who was in his own person God and man. Consequently all our knowledge of God, including our knowledge of him as creator, must begin with Jesus Christ and only with him.

(b) We can now see more clearly what Barth meant by the second half of the *Credo* sentence about God as creator, that this speaks not only of the freedom of God over against the world but also of his '*relationship* (one could also say: of His love) to the world'.[9] It is only because of the relationship between God and the world which he initiated in Jesus Christ that we are able to know him at all and say anything about him, even that he is creator of the world and our creator.

> What the meaning of God the Creator is and what is involved in the work of creation, is in itself not less hidden from us men than everything else that is contained in the Confession . . . It is not the case that the truth about God the Creator is directly accessible to us and that only the truth of the second article needs a revelation . . .
>
> By becoming man in Jesus Christ, the fact has also become plain and credible that God is the Creator of the world. We have no alternative source of revelation.[10]

It is therefore through God's act of grace in Jesus Christ that we know him as Father Almighty, maker of heaven and earth, but along with this comes the knowledge that creation in the beginning was already an act of grace. So while our knowledge of the grace of the creator-God may have begun with Jesus Christ, God's grace did not. It was there from the beginning.

This is the other side of the apparently harsh doctrine of the radical otherness of God which makes it possible for Barth to identify the freedom of God and the love of God as two aspects of his one relationship to the world. The freedom of the creator from his creation is sometimes taken to mean that such a God must be aloof and uncaring, but on the contrary, to say that God is free *and* that he is creator confirms his love in two ways. It points to a God who creates not because he has to, not out of some inner necessity, not because he is lonely and needs companionship, or is incomplete and needs to be fulfilled, not, in other words, for what he gets out of it, but just because he is gracious and in his generosity chooses to bring into existence and to sustain in being that which was not. More than this, he shows his love for what he creates by making it no mere extension of himself but something different, with its own distinct reality. When God looks at the creation and pronounces it 'good' this is no narcissistic sentiment; it is genuine appreciation of the value of that which is other than himself.

> Creation is grace: a statement at which we should like best to pause in reverence, fear and gratitude. God does not grudge the existence of the reality distinct from Himself; He does not grudge it its own reality, nature and freedom . . . We exist and heaven and earth exist in their complete, supposed infinity, because God gives them existence. That is the great statement of the first article.[11]

Yet it is still consistent to maintain that God is the one who 'remains hidden from us even in His revelation . . . Who, in disclosing Himself, conceals Himself, Who, in coming near to us, remains far from us, Who, in being kind to us, remains holy'.[12] He makes himself known but in ways that run counter to expectation. Because he is other, our reason remains incapable of grasping him and comprehending who he is. He can therefore be recognized only by faith which holds to what reason dismisses as scandalous.

In a Christmas sermon preached in 1533 Luther exemplified the power and persuasiveness of the approach described here, holding to the otherness of God, the impossibility of coming to know him by spinning theories of our own, the love of God who gives himself to us, the unexpectedness of the way he chooses, the need for faith to recognize what he has done:

> O what a ridiculous thing that the one true God, the high majesty should be made man; that here they should be joined, man and his Maker, in one person. Reason opposes this with all its might. Here then those wise thoughts with which our reason soars upward toward heaven to seek out God in his own Majesty, and to probe out how he reigns there on high, are taken from us. The goal is fixed elsewhere so that I should run from all the corners of the world to Bethlehem . . . yes, that subdues the reason. Do not seek what is too high for thee. But here it comes down before my eyes so that I can see the babe there in His Mother's lap. There lies a human being who was born like any other child, and lives like any other child and shows no other nature, manner and work than any other human being, so that no heart could guess that the creature is the Creator . . . Reason must bow and confess her blindness in that she wants to climb to heaven to fathom the divine while she cannot see what lies before her eyes.[13]

3. *Creation and Fall*

It is not difficult to anticipate how the doctrine of man and the fall will look from this viewpoint. To say that man is made in the image of God cannot mean that he is a model of God, or that he has the spark of divinity in his human clay, or that some likeness of the divine in him provides the point of contact between man and God. Therefore, 'made in the image of God' is interpreted as 'made with the responsibility of imaging God', that is, of reflecting him in the world, standing in the same relationship to the world as he stands to us. This preserves the creator-creature otherness because when people image or reflect God they no more possess God's nature than a mirror possesses the object that it reflects. The two remain quite distinct. Consequently the fall is seen as the attempt on our part to disregard this creator-creature relationship, or, more precisely, to rebel against what we take to be subservient status. This does not explain the origin of evil, of course,[14] but it does point to what lies behind all evil human actions. In expounding Genesis 3 Barth maintained that the creature neither could nor should be God, but this is the fundamental human sin – we try to usurp the authority of the creator. We try on our own account to judge between good and evil. Attempting to overcome the threatening chaotic forces we look to our own capacities instead of to the power of God, and consequently we ourselves are overcome by those very forces. In this turning away from the creator we no longer reflect him; nothing of his image remains.[15] We think we are acting in freedom but are selling ourselves into slavery. We contribute to the chaos of a world without God.

Barth makes it clear that such actions are directed not only at man but at God. They amount to robbery and rebellion. They are characteristic of the whole human situation, but they are also personal because we make them our own:

Clearly – and this lies already in the word 'Fall' – God is here deserted and denied by men; He suffers and is robbed . . . a robbery which becomes apparent in our arrogant endeavour to cross the line of death by which we are bounded; in our drunken blurring of the distance which separates us from God; in our forgetfulness of his invisibility; in our investing of man with the form of God and of God with the form of man; and in our devotion to some romantic infinity, some 'No-God' of this world, which we have created for ourselves . . . In its concrete form sin is no more than the ever-widening appearance and the expression and abounding in time of this Original Fall. But there is also another invisible significance attaching to sin. It is *ungodliness and unrighteousness* of men, since it damages the living relationship between God and man, and appropriates to itself the madness of the devil – ye shall be as God.[16]

However, standing by himself in this way man does not even know that he is fallen and headed for disaster. Knowledge of himself as sinful creature as well as knowledge of God as Father and creator comes only in Jesus Christ. In Christ he sees the humility, obedience and truth of the one genuinely human being; only then and by contrast does he recognize the dimensions of his own sin – his pride in wanting to exalt himself to the level of God, his sloth which lets him sink into the mire of anxiety and inhumanity, his falsehood which rejects the truth of grace.[17]

4. *New Creation in Jesus Christ*

The lines of construction for a picture of new creation have already been drawn. In this approach creation and fall are interpreted largely in terms of history and of the God-man relationship, and the same is true of new creation which is seen as the fulfilment of God's purpose which he has had for humankind from the beginning. And just as our knowledge of God as creator and of ourselves as sinners depends on Jesus Christ, so new creation has its beginning and end in him as well.

The beginning of this new creation must, of course, be God's initiative, not man's. As creature man is to find fulfilment not in any inevitable development of his creaturely nature but through something additional, through grace, the gift of the creator-God. Man has turned his back on this gift, thereby disrupting his relationship to God, cutting the ground from under his own feet, and losing his whole *raison d'être*. To revert to a familiar metaphor, the gulf between the creator and the creature is now seen to have an additional dimension –- to the initial structural one of otherness is now added the dynamic one of rebellion. A bridge can be built out only from the side of God, but man is neither willing nor able to secure it from his side, so God needs to stand with man as well to complete the work. Just this was achieved in Jesus Christ, the God-man. Already in him creature and creator have come together; God and man are reconciled in him:

> Reconciliation as the restoration of the communion of sinful men with God in Christ is certainly complete . . . Whoever is in Christ, *is* a new creature: the old has gone; behold, it *is* become new! . . . But all in *faith*. In faith, the full consummation of our communion with Christ exists here and now.[18]

So the first phase of new creation, reconciliation in Jesus Christ, is already here. The final phase, redemption, has yet to come, but that too will be achieved by God through Jesus Christ. What has yet to be,

> redemption is reconciliation without qualification, without the 'not-yet' which we must here and now combine with the 'in Christ' . . . For redemption in its true strict sense we *wait*. And Redeemer in this true, strict sense is Jesus Christ in his second coming – not before and not other-wise . . . If now redemption is, viewed positively, the actualization of the destined nature of man (which has not been forfeited but frustrated by sin) in a new creation . . . its abode is not with us but with God; not on this side of, but beyond, the resurrection of the dead.[19]

So the new creation begins and ends with God's action in his Son. It comprises the reconciliation achieved in his incarnation, obedient life, death and resurrection, and the redemption which, in the second coming and final resurrection, will fulfil in actuality what is now anticipated in faith, the nature of man which the creator willed from the beginning.

5. *Implications: Between Redemption and Reconciliation*

This conclusion about the creation-fall-new-creation relationship certainly does justice to what we have seen of the biblical writers' concern to read the creative work of God in terms of covenant history and to understand the new creation in terms of Jesus' fulfilment of the covenant and anticipation of the end of the age. However, this still leaves questions about other aspects of biblical witness that may not be so well covered and about what implications follow for living in the created world between the times of reconciliation and redemption.

(a) *The creator-creation distinction.* We have already noted that affirming the discontinuity between the creator and his creation can provide valuable guidelines for involvement in the life of the world. Knowing that God is creator gives us hope that there is some purpose in natural and historical processes and therefore that there is some point to our participation. The world did not come about by chance nor do events occur at random, so it becomes worth our while to look for meaning and to shape our actions accordingly, especially since the creation has been given its own independent existence. This affirms the secular integrity of the world and our freedom within it because, according to the creator's intention, the world is not divine and is therefore open, available to be used. It no longer stands over against man, giving rise to superstitious fear and making necessary rituals to placate the nature-gods, to woo their favour and tap their power. We are set free to probe, test and inquire, to gain knowledge and to develop the science and technology that makes use of the world and its resources. We are given freedom from the gods of history too, from the false claims of any person or institution in the world that poses as divine, demanding allegiance from us that can belong only to the creator. This provides the ground on which we can refuse to give any of the worldly powers our ultimate allegiance and from which we can make a critical appraisal of their place in God's creative purpose.

All this is to the good. It can, however, lead to a *de facto* conservatism. What begins as a refusal to give divine status to the institutions of society can become a denial of their importance, a reluctance to have anything to do with them, and consequently a tacit endorsement of things as they are. It may also lead to involvement on purely pragmatic grounds, for what begins as a refusal to acknowledge God in society can become a denial that his will for society can ever be found, and then involvement takes place without any serious attempt to discover a theological basis for it. I think that Barth himself illustrates the point. During the nineteen-twenties when he was still giving priority to the gulf between God and man and had not yet made the bridging of the gulf his theological starting-point, he was able to write that 'world-history is characterized by a pervasive monotony; politics and political questions are fundamentally un-interesting'.[20] Emphasizing that the Church should take a critical and iconoclastic stand against culture he maintained that society and our involvement in it must always be at a second level of reality. In 1926 he wrote:

> With this eschatological anticipation, the Church confronts society . . . not as a spoilsport, but in the knowledge that art and science, business and politics, techniques and education are really a game – a serious game, but a game, and *game* means an imitative and ultimately ineffective activity – the significance of which lies not in its attainable goals but in what it signifies. And the game might actually be played better and more successfully, the more it was recognized as a game. *Our* earnestness could not be im-paired by making it clear to ourselves that the game can never be ultimately serious, and never is; that the right

and the possibility of being wholly in earnest is God's alone.[21]

A few years later found Barth opposing Hitler with far more earnestness than was warranted by any view of politics as a game, even a serious game. He had come to see in Nazi Germany not just an 'imitative and ultimately ineffective activity' but an actual incarnation of the demonic. He became, somewhat to his own surprise, a leading figure in the Church's opposition to Hitler, but there is some reason to think that his courageous stand was at first based more on an intuitive revulsion to what was happening than on conclusions drawn from his theology as formulated up to that time. Before the Nazis began to bring pressure to bear on the churches Barth was prepared to follow a policy of co-existence, and his opposition began only when the state imposed restrictions on the churches and on preaching, restrictions which some Christians were prepared to support. It developed further with the anti-Semitic pogrom which Barth repudiated as a persecution of the people of God and therefore as a blasphemous denial of his grace. After that the pressures built up more and more, and Barth's critical attitude to the régime did find sound theological expression in the Barmen Declaration of the Confessing Church, asserting as it did that God's creative presence could be seen only by beginning with Jesus Christ and not with supposed manifestations of divine power in the blood, race and soil of the nation. Nevertheless, after he was forced to leave Germany and as Hitler's invasions continued, Barth's opposition was sometimes expressed in terms that ignored his own theological strictures against equating any human activity with the work of God. In one famous letter, for example, he maintained that every Czech soldier who took up arms against the Nazis was fighting for Christ and his Church. His post-war refusal to support the resistance to the Soviet invasion of Hungary in the same terms, which made

Reinhold Niebuhr so angry, may have reflected more than a reluctance, as Barth put it, to be on the side either of Mr Truman or the Pope. It may have been a return to a political stand more in keeping with his earlier theology.

The relationship between Barth's theology, his theory of social ethics and his actual political decisions is a complicated one which has been subjected to extended scrutiny.[22] I introduced it simply because it tends to confirm that a theological approach such as Barth's of the nineteen-twenties can lead to an engagement with politics only from a critical distance, and that when someone with that viewpoint does become actively involved he is likely to do so in ways that neglect or even run counter to that theological stand. Further confirmation may be found in Luther's contrasting attitudes toward the ecclesiastical authority of Rome and the secular power of the Princes. He found theological grounds for resisting one but not the other. An emphasis on the radical effects of the fall led Luther to conclude that the Christian could not participate in secular government without compromising his status as redeemed. This resulted in his condoning and finally actively supporting an oppressive system. When Luther formulated his theology of the cross in opposition to the prevailing theology of glory he was quite prepared to extend this into a practical attack on the mediaeval Church, but he was not prepared to make it the basis for criticizing the structure of feudal society. When he did intervene in secular affairs during the Peasants' Revolt he moved, as Moltmann has recently observed, to quite different theological ground.

> What he wrote to the peasants did not express the critical and liberating force of the cross, the choosing of the lowly which puts the mighty to shame, nor the polemic of the crucified God against pride and subjection, domination and slavery, but instead a non-Protestant mysticism of suffering and humble submission.[23]

(b) *The concentration on Jesus Christ as new creation.* Although this gives cohesion to various aspects of the approach we have been considering, the results can be unnecessarily restrictive in two ways. The scope for human initiative and response may be minimized and the value of the non-human sphere of creation down-graded.

Even when it is insisted that the reconciliation effected by God still has to be appropriated by man, and that we should not rest content because the final fulfilment is still in the future, this can be regarded as little more than signing a document someone else has drawn up, going through an exercise whose issue is never in doubt. Living between the times of reconciliation and redemption can be seen as just the necessary but predictable outworking of what is, in effect, over and done with. Reconciliation in Jesus Christ is already achieved; redemption is a foregone conclusion because it is all the work of God in which we play no more part than we did at the creation. We will have no more to do with the second coming of Christ than with the first. New creation belongs to a history which is not the history of the world but a special history of the saving work of God. We are involved only as beneficiaries of a process which takes place in another order of reality, like heirs to a fortune bequeathed by a remote relation in an unknown country.

This is a caricature of Barth's views rather than a description, but perhaps retaining something of a caricature's capacity to show up tendencies in bold relief. In Barth's theology, which is representative of the transcendentalist approach, the scene of God's action tends to be scaled down from the whole of the created order to human history, then to the narrower history of the Judeo-christian tradition, and then to a mysterious history of divine activity that stands behind (although it cannot be identified with) the history of Israel and the Church. Not that Barth suggests that God's concern narrows down in that way; on the contrary, of course, he insists that the creator-God holds in his care the whole of creation. But by insisting at the same time that our knowledge of God must begin with Jesus Christ and that new creation is focussed in him, the scope of theological interest is effectively restricted to the relation between God and his human creatures. When it is asserted further that knowledge of man as well as of God must begin with Jesus Christ, interest is limited still more because when we look to him as God-man in order to see what genuine humanity is we concentrate on what is unique about him – that he embodies the restored image of God. True human-ness is then under-stood not as something that Jesus shares with the rest of the created world but as something he does not, as something that belongs to him alone, the fulness of new creation.

To press a little further the point that Barth's approach discourages theological attention to the non-human creation. We have already seen that for Barth's early theology the main point about the doctrine of creation was that it affirmed the otherness of God, his distance from the creation. All that could then be said about the world had to be put in negatives – it is not God, it has its separate reality but is still dependent on the creator for continued existence, it cannot sustain man in his rebellion against God. The world of nature figured in the new creation only as the location for the time being of man who is being renewed. In his famous commentary on Romans, for example, Barth was able to make very little of chapter 8, verses 19–22. Wherever possible he placed the emphasis on man as fallen creature waiting for revelation and redemption rather than on the whole created universe longing for its release. When he did consider 'the whole creation groaning and in travail' he turns attention im-mediately from the wider context back to man, even to man's knowledge:

The whole creation! Yes, even that which has been hidden and submerged, and so made more difficult of access to our knowledge! Our knowledge itself! for we know that what we know and shall know is a thing loosed from its Primal origin, a relative thing separated from the absolute by an abyss.[24]

The natural world and the other creatures provide only the incidental backdrop to the all-important drama of God and man.

In Barth's later theology the place given to the created order other than man becomes no greater. Its incidental status is in a way confirmed by the place given to Jesus Christ because although the starting-point for this later theology is the overcoming of the creator-creature gap rather than the gap itself, the effects of the overcoming are spelled out almost exclusively in human terms. More than that, the centrality given to Christ in the *Church Dogmatics* includes a new way of emphasizing the grace of God that weakens Barth's earlier proclamation of the creation as God's free act of grace *par excellence*. In the *Dogmatics* Barth posited an act of God's grace that preceded the creation, namely the election of Jesus Christ before time and us in him. By giving priority in this way to the election of humanity rather than to the creation of the world Barth has actually increased the emphasis on man, and the rest of the created order becomes even more dependent and derivative than before. For this reason Barth is able to say that the theological doctrine of the creature is, in practice, anthropology or the doctrine of man. It also enables him to conclude that while man lives in the world as a neighbour of the animals and even of the plants and other living things, this must remain a silent theological presupposition for we can have 'no certain information concerning the unity of our life with the life outside of us'.[25] By thus consigning the relationship between man and nature to the darkness Barth leaves us with insufficient theological light to lead us through the ecological gloom that hangs over us.[26]

However, I do not think that Barth's silence about the

rest of creation necessarily follows from the transcendentalist approach, nor do I think that this approach leads necessarily to undervaluing or exploiting nature. In fact it has some features that help us to face the ecological crisis. It is, I believe, essential to have an understanding of man such as this approach provides in order to recognize the full dimensions of the crisis and to be realistic about possible lines of action. We need to recognize, for example, the radical effects of the fall, the extent and tenacity of human selfishness and capacity for self-destruction in order realistically to assess our situation and the possibilities ahead of us. Only then can we begin to appreciate the radical nature and the wide-ranging scope of the changes needed if we are to live responsibly in creation, and if future generations are to live in it at all. This is not going to happen simply by drawing attention to the problem and waiting for awareness to lead to rational planning and sharing. Human exploitation of nature through squandering and destruction of its resources is not just careless disregard, a childish shortsightedness not yet outgrown. It is a participation in evil, a rebellion against the call to be responsible for creation, a rebellion against God which is also an attack upon our neighbours, gratifying our own desires and callously disregarding the needs of others now and in the future. Nothing less than a radical change of heart and of the way we live and make decisions as societies and nations can give any hope for the future of the world, and we need to listen to Barth's insistence that this cannot happen without the gracious initiative of the creator-God.

6. Ontological: Paul Tillich

Imagine an approach to the doctrine of creation from exactly the opposite point of the theological compass from the one just considered. Its impetus would come from a sense of continuity rather than discontinuity. It would affirm a positive relationship between God and the world, infinite and finite, eternal and changing, revelation and reason, divine and human, religion and culture, theology and philosophy. It could be an imaginary construct dreamed up by negating the main features of the transcendentalist, but is in fact the approach followed consistently by Paul Tillich, although he was the first to acknowledge its dependence upon idealism.[1]

The word he chose to describe his method was *correlation*, whose purpose is to explain 'the contents of the Christian faith through existential questions and theological answers in mutual interdependence'.[2] These existential questions arise out of our everyday experiences, but they are most likely to receive their correlative answer when they are linked to the experiences of others and consequently seen as features of a larger human situation. In this wider and deeper analysis of the situation material comes from the whole spectrum of human reflection on experience, from the various art forms for example, and from the disciplines of psychology, philosophy and sociology. It is the task of the theologian to bring these insights into creative relationship with the content of faith, to correlate, as Tillich puts it, the questions implied in the human situation with the answers present in the christian message.

But how can we know that such a method will work? How can we be sure that the arts and sciences can genuinely analyze and display the human situation? Why will the questions so shaped find corresponding answers in the Gospel? All this is possible only if we can count on some underlying reality that already links the human situation and the divine Word, and on some correspondence between thought and being so that the way we think about things does in some way match the way they really are. This Tillich recognized, and in his *Systematic Theology* he made it quite clear that the discussion of theological method which came in the Introduction assumed a view of being and reality which was spelled out only later, in Part II.[3] Correlation, he acknowledged, was a concept derived from a prior knowledge of the whole system, and at the heart of that system, logically prior to everything else, was his ontology.

1. Starting-point: Being and its Ground

One of the most difficult things about understanding and describing Tillich's approach is to know where to start. A discussion of his theological method depends upon knowing about his ontology, yet the way he discusses ontology is shaped by the method he has chosen. He says that knowledge must begin with experience, yet experience is already being influenced by the way we think about it and the terms we use to describe it. Only reason is capable of plumbing the depths of being, yet reason itself depends upon its 'ontological foundation'. However, the very circularity of this argument which makes it difficult to know where to start also guarantees that any chosen starting-point will sooner or later give access to the whole. So we will begin with what for Tillich has logical priority, his view of being.

Everything that is participates in being, but what makes human experience unique is the awareness of this participation that relates us to everything else that is. We know that we are; we know that we live in relationship to others but that we are not they; we know that we depend upon the environment of the world but that we are not simply identical with that world. This is the basic truth about reality which Tillich calls the *structure of being*. Our awareness of this structure begins with our consciousness of this involvement with, yet separation from, the world. It continues as reason works on the implications of this awareness: Why do we experience this as both joy and pain? Why is being a self experienced both as exhilarating independence and as harrowing estrangement? Will we be our true selves by enlarging the area of independence or by restricting it? Is our destiny in reunion or more radical separation? And our awareness of the structure of being is completed as the questions thus formulated meet with their correlative answers.

> Man occupies a pre-eminent position in ontology, not as an outstanding object among other objects, but as that being who asks the ontological question and in whose self-awareness the ontological answer can be found . . . [He] is able to answer the ontological question himself because he experiences directly and immediately the structure of being and its elements.[4]

The structure of being that is revealed by this awareness and questioning is the self-world relationship. Along with the recognition of ourselves as 'selves' comes awareness of the world to which we belong but which is not a mere extension or projection of ourselves. This sounds straightforward enough, but its complexity begins to emerge when the meaning of 'self' and of 'world' in this relationship is explored a little further. All living beings, Tillich maintains, have self-hood to some extent, but 'being a self' he reserves for humans who are alone aware of their self-hood. Other things and beings have an environment in which they live and with which they interact, but only humans are able to reflect on this interaction and thus to organize their experience with this environment. Only then can this environment be called a 'world'. Therefore neither self nor world in this basic ontological structure is a simple entity, a discrete object among others. The self is a complex entity made up of experience, interaction and reflection. The world is a cosmos, not just 'the sum total of all beings'[5] but an organized and unified whole whose principle of organization is accessible to human reflection. Consequently each term depends upon the other for its reality and meaning. 'The interdependence of ego-self and world is the basic ontological structure and implies all others. Both sides of the polarity are lost if either side is lost. The self without a world is empty; the world without a self is dead.'[6]

Basic as this ontological structure is to Tillich's system there is something even more fundamental on which the structure is built. This begins to show up as the question 'How is this possible?' is put to the self-world polarity. What makes a self a 'self' is, as we saw, the capacity to reflect on awareness and experience. But what makes this reflection possible? What makes the environment into a 'world' is its integrity and order, but how is such an order possible? Their inter-relatedness makes both self and world real, but how is such inter-relatedness possible? Tillich gives the same answer to each of these questions: reason.

> Reason makes the self a self, namely, a centred structure; and reason makes the world a world, namely, a structured whole. Without reason, without the *logos* of being, being would be chaos, that is, it would not be being but only the possibility of it. But where there is reason there are a self and a world in interdependence. The function of the self in which it actualizes its rational structure is the mind, the bearer of subjective reason. Looked at by the mind, the world is reality, the bearer of objective reason.[7]

It is obviously true that the world appears chaotic until we bring our reason to bear on it, applying, for example, the principle of cause and effect to events in nature and history, but Tillich is driving at something deeper than that. We are able to find order in the chaos, finding at the same time a self and a world, because order is already there, and because the order that is there in the world is congruent with the order that is ourselves. When we make sense of the world we do so not by imposing our own alien pattern of thinking upon it but by discovering the same rational scheme of things there that is also in us. That is why the self can be called 'subjective reason' and the world 'objective reason'.

We may now be inclined to think that this is as far as speculation can take us, yet the question 'why?' can still be put, and when it is another ontological level comes to light. Why this congruence of pattern between self and world? Where does it come from? Some philosophers are content to say, 'That's the way reality is.' Tillich is not yet quite ready to pull the shutters down. He acknowledges that the answer cannot be extrapolated from our experience nor conjured up by reason working on that experience:

> The basic ontological structure cannot be derived. It must be accepted. The question, 'What precedes the duality of self and world, of subject and object?' is a question in which reason looks into its own abyss – an abyss in which distinction and derivation disappear.[8]

There is, nevertheless, an answer, an answer that comes from revelation. The inter-relation and inter-dependence of self and world derive from their common source, the ground of being in which they both participate.

2. Creator and Creature

> The doctrine of creation is not the story of an event which took place 'once upon a time'. It is the basic description of the relation between God and the world.[9]

With this Barth would have agreed, but he was fundamentally at odds with Tillich's view of what that relation is. For Barth, to say that God is creator was another way of asserting his otherness, the radical discontinuity between God and his creation. For Tillich it points instead to their continuity, to 'the situation of creatureliness and to its correlate, the divine creativity'.

(a) *God's creativity*. This view of God as creator is obviously shaped by Tillich's ontology. It is, in effect, an elaboration of what he has already said about the structure of being and its ground in God as being-itself. Each of the aspects of ontology considered in the previous section depended, as we saw, upon the continuity between God and the world, so if the doctrine of creation is, as Tillich contends, a description of that relation then it must re-assert that continuity. Theology itself depends upon it because correlation is the method of theology and that is possible only if there is a positive relationship between the two sides. Revelation can come as the answer to questions raised by human experience only because the two are not disparate; both derive from the divine ground of being and are thus fundamentally in tune with one another. In the same way, self and world are inter-related as subjective and objective reason, and reason in its own depths is grounded in being-itself. Therefore to speak of God as creator is not to point to one attribute that he has among many, nor to one activity among others in which he engages. It is simply another way of speaking about his continuing relation to the world. 'The divine life and the divine creativity are not different. God is creative because he is God.'[10]

There are three aspects to this creativity of God, corresponding symbolically to past, present and future – which Tillich calls originating, sustaining and directing creativity. *Originating creativity* cannot just deal with what happened at the beginning since Tillich denies that the doctrine of creation is about an event that happened in time or at the outset of time, so he uses it to reiterate the meaning of the traditional *creatio ex nihilo*. He reinforces the line of demarcation that this lays down between Christianity and paganism or any other form of ultimate dualism, agreeing with the traditional view that God does not create by drawing on any 'given' nor by warding off opposing forces for this would make him less than ultimate. As creator he is alone in being the ultimate source of all that is. However, Tillich goes on to maintain a positive purpose for the *ex nihilo* doctrine in addition to this critical or protective one. Not only does it deny dualism, it affirms something about creatureliness, namely, that creatureliness is necessarily finite because it comes out of nothing and therefore retains a 'heritage of non-being'.[11] In other words, creatureliness is inevitably limited in length and scope, but since these limitations are part of what makes creatureliness what it is they are not themselves tragic. They give rise to tragedy only when we refuse to accept them as part of creatureliness, trying to transcend finitude by our own efforts, or withdrawing in disappointment from active participation in life because of its limitations.

Sustaining creativity is the term Tillich uses for the continuing relation of God to the world and for the world's continuing dependence upon him. Traditionally this has been understood as God's 'preservation' of the world, which allows for the ironical situation that a creature has freedom to rebel against the creator only because the creator still provides him with life and thus with capacity to rebel. Resisting interpretations of this which allow God only to begin the process and then abdicate (deism), or to invade it on occasion from the outside (theistic deism), or simply to be identified with it (pantheism), Tillich insists that preservation is 'continuous creativity, in that God out of eternity creates things and time together . . . He is creative in every moment of temporal existence, giving the power of being to everything that has being out of the creative ground of the divine life.'[12] Since God's creativity is 'continuous' there is necessarily a continuity between originating and sustaining creativity, but they still need to be distinguished, not just to achieve neatness in the theoretical system but to dispel anxiety in the face of bewildering changes. In this sense we need the doctrine of creation in the same way that the Israelites did, not to complete a pattern of thought nor even to convey information about the beginning of things but in order to face with hope the threatening present. Originating creativity is not much help to us at that point. It affirms that God created out of nothing, emphasizing the independence of God and the absolute newness of what he creates, but that does little to alleviate our anxiety. It may help us to stand in awe of the greatness of God, but that does not in itself provide a dependable basis for thought and action in the present.

These days we face not only the disintegration of the particular things on which people have relied – this nation or that, this ideology or the other, this currency or economic system or resource or invention – but also a threat to the very foundations on which these particular strongholds have been built. Technology is called in question; the continuity of human civilization is threatened; the regenerating capacity of nature itself is in jeopardy. What we need is an assurance of continuity within the turmoil, an assurance that is not superficial but comes from the depths of being itself, and that is what sustaining creativity provides – the given structures of reality which continue within all the changes and which in fact give direction to the changes, the lines of construction within which God's power to sustain his creation now moves, 'the regular and calculable in things' as Tillich puts it. 'The faith in God's sustaining creativity is the faith in the continuity of the structure of reality as the basis for being and acting.'[13]

This continuity should not, however, be seen as merely keeping things the way they always have been. The lines of construction are open to the future so that God's creativity is moving toward fulfilment. This future dimension Tillich calls *directing creativity*, whose aim is to 'fulfil in actuality what is beyond potentiality and actuality in the divine life . . . to drive every creature toward such a fulfilment'.[14] This aspect of God's activity is usually called Providence, and at its best the doctrine retains its paradoxical character, affirming that despite appearances to the contrary there is meaning to life and history. Faith recognizes what reason misses for lack of evidence; it sees victory in what the world counts as defeat; it holds to the cross as the meaning of history. Some interpretations of Providence, however, both secular and religious, have attempted to increase its rationality by diminishing the paradoxical, reducing God's role to that of spectator who knows everything but does nothing about what is to happen, or of puppeteer who does everything to make sure that things go according to plan. We are then left with God eliminated from the world so that man can be free, or with man whose freedom is eliminated so that God's will for the world can prevail. Tillich proposes instead a view which does not set the freedom of man and the will of God in opposition, which allows for the ultimate destiny of man to be fulfilled despite the apparently blind alleys of error and meaninglessness and estrangement into which man's freedom leads him. Directing creativity makes use of whatever situations arise, and from these builds towards our future fulfilment.

> All existential conditions are included in God's directing creativity. They are not increased or decreased in their power, nor are they cancelled. Providence is not interference; it is creation. It uses all factors, both those given by freedom and those given by destiny, in creatively directing everything toward its fulfilment.[15]

(b) *Human creatureliness.* As we saw earlier, Tillich holds that the doctrine of creation refers to human creatureliness and its correlate, divine creativity. In discussing the latter we have inevitably included the former, but one more point needs to be made if we are to do justice to Tillich's view. With his understanding of the correlation between creativity and creatureliness, divine and human, his interpretation of man as image of God is bound to be very different from that of Barth. In fact he uses the *imago dei* with far-reaching implications not only for the doctrines of God and man but also for Christology. In a few sentences of fundamental importance Tillich asserts that man is able positively to reflect the being of God, that he does so because his rational structure is analogous to God's, and that it is just this analogous structure that provides the conditions for an incarnation of the divine within the fully human.

> Man is the image of God in that in which he differs from all other creatures, namely, his rational structure. Of course, the term 'rational' is subject to many misinterpretations . . . Man is the image of God because in him the ontological elements are complete and united on a creaturely basis, just as they are complete and united in God as the creative ground. Man is the image of God because his *logos* ₋ analogous to the divine *logos*, so that the divine *logos* can a₋ ₋ear as man without destroying the humanity of man.[16]

What are these 'ontological elements' which, in their completeness, make man what he is? They are three pairs of apparently opposite features within whose polarity the being of man finds its reality. Put in a slightly different way, man *is* the relation of these elements in tension, the elements of individualization and participation, dynamics and form, freedom and destiny. Man is, for example, identifiable as a self and experiences himself as different from everything else that is. He is an *individual*, but is able to be so only in relation to other people and things, and is conscious of his individuality only because he *participates* in that which is other than himself and can therefore recognize it as the other. Genuine individuality is possible only when there is full participation, and in the human being this comes to its fulfilment in a community of persons. The same creative tension is seen between the elements of *dynamics and form*. That which is completely static has no vitality. Movement and change are an integral part of life without which there can be no self-hood, yet there must be something that remains constant throughout the change otherwise there would only be a succession of discrete states of being rather than a self that was changing. Out of the polar relation between the dynamic that allows for transcendence and the form that guarantees conservation, the self comes to be.

Freedom and destiny are the polar elements in which the others find their possibility and fulfilment. Man is able to be an individual who participates in community rather than an object set in its surroundings because he is free. His self-hood grows because he is able to choose and to live with the results of his choices. Yet there is also a dimension of the given and the consequent which points to the destiny that is in polar tension with freedom, for man can only choose from among the possibilities that are presented to him, and, once he has chosen, his influence over the outcome is strictly limited, although he remains free to face his destiny as he will.

3. *Existence and Fall*

This description of man as the image of God, drawing his being from God the ground of being, reflecting in the harmonious structure of his being the divine *logos*, is a description of ideal or essential human being, not human beings as they are. Our actual life, or, as Tillich calls it, human life under the conditions of existence, is very different. In the life that we know we are constantly threatened with the possibility of becoming nothing, and in our resulting anxiety we try to make sure of ourselves by affirming one aspect of our being or another. But then the tension that is characteristic of the polar elements in our essential being is broken. Without its appropriate counter-balance each aspect of our being becomes distorted and we ourselves are torn apart. The main features of essential being remain (the ontological elements) but because unchecked by their correlates they go beyond bounds and become destructive parodies of what they should be. Individuality, for instance, without participation in community becomes loneliness. Participation without individuality becomes collectivism. Dynamics when taken out of double harness with form becomes an unbridled chaos which eventually loses its own power because forces pulling in opposite directions cancel each other out. Form without the dynamic that provides a creative intention becomes empty, sterile, and finally dead. Freedom cut loose from destiny becomes arbitrary, aimless and finally pointless. Destiny without freedom leads to resignation in the face of an equally oppressive fate.

That describes us as we are, but why have we come to this? Tillich has a two-level answer. The first, an existential one, we have already looked at. It points to anxiety as the root of the problem. Being finite we are faced with the possibility of becoming nothing and that possibility we feel as threat, but in struggling against it we fall apart. The second is an ontological one, and it begins to show through when we persist with the question 'why?' Why is our present existence a struggle against the threat of non-being? The answer, already programmed by the system's ontological input, is that this is an inevitable consequence of our finitude. The anxiety that goes with the disruption of our own being is due, according to Tillich, to the prior disruption between our being and its ground, a disruption which must accompany the move from essential being to existential being because that is what coming into existence *is* – a move out of our grounding in being-itself. So creation itself becomes a fall from essential being into existence and must involve distortion and disruption, a view which owes more to the neo-Platonic understanding of the built-in deficiencies of the world than to the biblical account of its original goodness.

For Tillich, then, the doctrines of creation and fall coalesce at the point of man's creatureliness. 'Fully developed creatureliness', he says, 'is fallen creatureliness'; not just in fact (which would be consistent with the view that all people are sinners) but necessarily and in principle because the creature has to step outside the creative ground of the divine life if his essence is to be actualized in existence. Estrangement is therefore more than a universal characteristic of the creature; it is part of the process of creation itself.

4. *New Being and New Creation*

As we saw in chapter 4, the biblical witness to new creation takes some account of the whole of the natural order but focuses on the meaning of this new creation for man in the context of history. The creative act of God at the beginning is linked to the consummating event at the end, and the part that Jesus plays is decisive. The approach typified by Tillich takes account of all these features but gives them a characteristic interpretation in line with the ontological groundwork already laid.

In our present experience of life 'under the conditions of existence' the effects of new creation can be known, and they amount to the restoration of our creaturely being as far as the limits of finitude will allow. We are reunited with our divine ground, at the same time finding that the destructive disruption within our own self-hood is being overcome. This, according to Tillich, is achieved through the power of love which brings about 'the reunion with that to which one belongs and from which one is estranged'.[17] That is what love does, and there is no further definition of love possible. Love *is* the reuniting power that goes with new being. It puts us into that relationship with the divine ground of our being that enables us more fully to appropriate the sustaining creativity of God. At the same time it renews our own being by restoring the balance between the ontological elements. Through reuniting love, for example, loneliness is overcome, self-assertion is damped down and genuine participation in community becomes possible. The anarchy of formless dynamic is dispelled as love gives new direction and purpose. Love sets limits to licence and so brings freedom under purposive control.

This is the new creation brought about by the power of reuniting love, but in the present this can be experienced only fragmentarily. For the 'final conquest of the ambiguities of life'[18] we must look forward to the end of history. In keeping with his interpretation of the symbols of creation and fall as the move from essence to existence, the fulfilment of new creation to come at the end of history will be the overcoming of existence in essence. And in line with the essential continuity between God and man, this fulfilment of new being is the final taking up of the human into the divine. New creation will then mean more than the overcoming of the disruption that is part of our present human experience; it will mean that our restored human being will be transformed into the eternal dimension. Human creativity and divine self-manifestation will be at one.

In this understanding of new creation Jesus Christ plays the definitive role, and Tillich presses the point that only where the identity between Jesus Christ and new creation is affirmed can there be a genuinely Christian statement of faith:

> Christianity is what it is through the affirmation that Jesus of Nazareth . . . is actually the Christ, namely, he who brings the new state of things, the New Being.[19]

To say that Jesus Christ is the New Being is to say that in him the ambiguities of life as we know them have been overcome. Although he lived under the conditions of existence his essential being was not disrupted or distorted, for through the power of love he remained rooted in the divine ground of being. This, Tillich said, is new in two ways: 'It is new in contrast to the merely potential character of essential being; and it is new over against the estranged character of existential being. It is actual, conquering the estrangement of actual existence.'[20] But to say that Jesus Christ is the new being is not just to say *that* this has occurred, but that it has occurred *in him*, in the kind of life that the New Testament portrays him as having lived. This was the test of faith that came to the disciples and which they almost failed: to recognize, contrary to what they had been expecting, that in the words and deeds and death of Jesus of Nazareth the new being was manifest. His was the life in which the power of new being shone through, as Tillich put it,

> first and decisively, as the undisrupted unity of the centre of his being with God; second, as the serenity and majesty of him who preserves this unity against all the attacks coming from estranged existence; and, third, as the self-surrendering love which represents and actualizes the divine love in taking the existential self-destruction upon himself.[21]

What has this new being in Jesus Christ to do with our being created anew? It is an anticipation of what is possible for us only at the end of history, but it has present force as well because to believe in Jesus Christ is not only to be assured that our new creation will be fulfilled, it is also to know the terms of that fulfilment. And to know that love is the principle of that fulfilment[22] is to be able to share it and so begin to live as a new creation:

> Inasmuch as Jesus as the Christ is a creation of the divine Spirit . . . so is he who participates in the Christ made into a new creature by the Spirit. The estrangement of his existential from his essential being is conquered in principle, i.e. in power and as a beginning.[23]

Although the terminology may be very different, the centrality of Jesus Christ is affirmed here as it was in the transcendentalist approach. Through him we know the power of new creation and look forward to its fulfilment; in him God and

man, divine ground and human existence, have come together. But whereas for Barth this was the great paradox,
the impossible possibility, the absolutely unique intersection
of divine and human, for Tillich, Jesus embodies what is in
principle open to all. Although in fact only in the picture of
Jesus as the Christ does essential godmanhood appear under
the conditions of existence without disruption and without
distortion, this does not stand as an affront to what reason
could expect. Given the starting-point of ontological continuity, the coming together of human and divine fits the
pattern that was laid out from the beginning. Jesus as the
Christ is not the one great paradox, he is the paradigm of
humanity in whom new being is manifest, available to all
who participate in it courageously, anticipating the fulfilment at the end of history.

5. *Appraisal*

(a) *Ontology and theology.* As a result of their diametrically
opposed approaches Barth and Tillich draw sharply contrasting conclusions about the doctrine of creation and the
related themes of fall and new creation. That much is clear.
What is not so clear is how to decide between the two since
each appears to the other to be building on shifting sand.
How can the dispute be settled when they disagree on what
makes for solid groundwork in the first place and then use
different formulae to calculate stresses and strains in the
structure itself?

     If one stands with Barth, for example, then every major
feature of Tillich's thought we have discussed so far will be
called into question. The basic idea of God as being-itself
in which all being is grounded will be rejected because it
conflicts with the view of God as creator of what is other than
himself. Consequently the whole ontological-theological
framework that Tillich set up is undermined. The method of
correlation must then be rejected because it wrongly assumes

a continuity between God, self and world, and between faith and reason. The view of God's image in man as *logos* congruent with the divine *logos* is impossible if there is no analogy of being between creator and creature. An understanding of the fall as inevitable distortion of essential being does not account for the dimension of wilful disobedience. The view of new creation as the overcoming of estrangement and final taking up of existence into essence depends too much on an inevitable world-process, too little on the initiative of God who effects radical transformation.

But why stand with Barth? It has become a convention to emphasize Barth's uncompromisingly biblical orientation and to contrast this with Tillich's dalliance with philosophy. Those who acknowledge the authority of the Bible are then expected to reject Tillich's approach because it is said that he uses the Bible only if he can make it illustrate conclusions drawn from a prior ontological system.[24] But even when Tillich's ontology is seen to permeate all his thought, to set this over against a 'biblical' view is a vast oversimplification. In the first place it fails to take account of the variety and development within the biblical witness itself, variety which shows that the biblical writers no less than twentieth-century theologians brought different perspectives to bear and put emphasis on different aspects of the tradition. In the canon of Law and Prophets, for instance, Israel's history was seen as the main arena in which God came to meet man, but in some later writing Wisdom has taken over as the medium through which God relates himself to man and the world. Consequently in the Wisdom literature the creation theme is seen in a different light. In Job 28, for example, reference to creation is made not, as in the prophetic tradition, to reinforce Israel's history with God, but in order to establish a more immediate individual relationship with God through Wisdom as God's agent of creation. In Proverbs 8 Wisdom herself proclaims her role in the creator's continuing involvement with his creation.

This simplistic Barth-Tillich contrast also overlooks the fact that the transcendentalist approach of the *Römerbrief* Barth, to which the accolade 'biblical' or the pejorative 'biblicist' are most commonly applied, was certainly narrowly selective in its biblical basis, and Barth himself has acknowledged that the grounds for selection were philosophically conditioned, at least in the negative sense of being chosen in order most effectively to refute prevailing philosophical theology. Therefore, despite his intention to give priority to the Bible Barth actually approached it with a framework already prepared, a view of creator and creation into which the biblical writings were pressed, distorting some and excluding others, so that however necessary it was to evict liberal theology the effect was to keep Schleiermacher in residence, although in the uncomfortable position of standing on his head.[25] Experience of man was still the source of knowledge of God, although now the experience of his otherness. Even when Barth began again with the overcoming of the creator-creature gulf in Jesus Christ as his starting-point, it could be argued that Tillich's views are more consistent with this premise than Barth's own. Once Barth came to insist that it is only in Jesus Christ that we can know God and man and their relationship, and that what we find in Jesus Christ is God and man united, why not agree with Tillich that the basic relationship between creator and creation is continuity rather than discontinuity?

This is not to suggest that Barth and Tillich were really saying the same thing. Of course they were not. For Tillich the incarnation was not the starting-point for understanding God and man but was a feasible conclusion from prior knowledge of a divine-human correlation, and this remains fundamentally at odds with Barth's view of the priority of God's revelation in Christ. Nevertheless, given the incarnation as starting-point this could have led to a view of the creator-creature relationship much closer to that of Tillich than

Barth himself allowed, even in later reflections such as his *Humanity of God.*[26]

(b) *Ontology and history.* In pointing to the difficulty of deciding between the approaches of Tillich and Barth I have not wanted to suggest that the only thing to do is to describe their views and leave it at that. Tillich himself acknowledges that the Bible is the basic source of systematic theology, and while that does not exclude other sources or demand an uncritical literalist interpretation it does indicate that his theological conclusions must be open to scrutiny in the light of the Bible which 'contains the original witness of those who participated in the revealing events'.[27] Do the symbols which he uses in correlating the answers of faith with the questions of existence adequately and genuinely reflect the biblical symbols? Do they convey what the biblical writers were really driving at?

To answer that would entail a full-scale study in its own right, but we ought to press it here, at least in relation to one of Tillich's conclusions already noted – the convergence of creation and fall. Some, seeing this convergence as an idealist or Platonist view of the world as less than real, reject it out of hand because it flatly contradicts the biblical view of God's creation as originally good, but that settles the issue a little too easily. Tillich certainly uses Platonist ideas, but he also reinterprets them, so unless all views that use non-biblical sources are to be excluded just on that ground the question of whether Tillich's conclusion is valid is still open, and we should pursue it further. Of course, if the biblical picture of the original goodness of creation is taken literally then that finishes the discussion. Tillich's idea of the convergence of creation and fall runs counter to that and is thereby cancelled out. But is it to be taken literally, any more than the ideas of a pre-fallen state of innocent humanity and harmonious nature? Those who accept the symbolic status of all of these, original goodness of creation and fall of Adam included, must also allow for their interpretation. We must then at least consider the possibility that Tillich's interpretation may adequately convey the meaning of the biblical symbols.

At one important point I think he does this far better than is generally acknowledged. In talking about the creation as a move from essence to existence with the inevitable distortions that result he does draw a distinction between finitude and tragedy. Both are universal characteristics of human existence, but while finitude is given with existence (being finite is what the creature *is*) tragedy is not. It may be universal and inevitable, and its possibility may be given to us with our freedom, but its actuality occurs only as we rebel against the limitations of our finitude. Traditionally, of course, only the rebellion and not the given finitude is labelled 'fall'[28] whereas Tillich uses it to cover both, but he clearly distinguishes the given and voluntary aspects. Consequently when he says that fully developed creatureliness is fallen creatureliness he does convey the biblical ideas both of the limitation involved in being a creature and the tragic consequences of using our freedom to rebel against that limitation. He also maintains the sense of our being free and yet driven, the ambiguous feeling conveyed by the biblical writers (and referred to in chapter 3) of being trapped by circumstances yet somehow responsible ourselves, in a way that is often missing in the more traditional interpretations.

More open to criticism is his use of the concept of 'non-being' in relation to creation, not just because it is 'unbiblical' but because it reduces the effectiveness of the distinction between finitude and tragedy just considered. He makes 'non-being' refer not to the absence of being but to some mysterious entity that has its own ontological status. The symbol of God's creating out of nothing does not then mean 'God does not create out of anything'; it means 'God did create out of something called non-being'. The systematic and logical difficulties that this entails have been discussed often enough and need no pursuing here, but I think it is worth commenting that it is this view more than the conflating of the terms 'creation' and 'fall' that leads to an underestimation of the reality of life in this world. By interpreting non-being not as an absence of being but as a negative principle that stands in dialectical relation to being, Tillich blunts the point of his own distinction between finitude and tragedy, for now the 'given' in creaturely existence is not just finitude but an infusion of non-being, not just limitation but the presence of a principle opposed to being, or at least standing over against it. To say that creaturely existence is finite is one thing; to say that it must 'take over the heritage of non-being' is another, and by equating the two (finitude unites being with dialectical non-being[29]) Tillich reduces the reality and significance of existence in the world, a reduction which may be compatible with his system but is not consistent with the biblical symbols.

Earlier in this chapter I quoted, with no critical comment at that stage, Tillich's view that 'the doctrine of creation is not the story of an event which took place "once upon a time". It is the basic description of the relation between God and the world.'[30] It is now worth recalling an observation from chapter 2, that the theologians responsible for the present shape of the Hexateuch took a different view. The doctrine of creation was, for them, both the story of an event and the basic description of the God-world relationship. It was the once-upon-a-time story that conveyed the basic description. To believe in God as creator was to rely upon his continuing relationship to the world, and it was just that relationship that was portrayed in story form, a relationship which gave to the history of men and of nations, past, present and future, a significance for which Tillich's re-interpretation does not allow. In the final estimate therefore I have to agree[31] with those who say that Tillich does not take history seriously enough, at least in the sense that his system allowed it only secondary status. This may seem an odd thing to say of a man whose involvement with socialism led to his exile from Germany, and whose writing so often dealt with social and political issues. Nevertheless, once he made non-being as well as finitude a necessary part of existence, his theological system could allow only a subordinate place to human history and could look for its fulfilment not within history nor at its climax but only in some realm above and beyond it:

> As a Christian theologian I would say that fulfilment is going on in every moment here and now beyond history, not some time in the future but here and now above ourselves . . . Something might happen which is elevated out of time into eternity. This is then a non-Utopian and true fulfilment of the meaning of history and of our own individual life.[32]

(c) *Ontology and ecology.* John Macquarrie in his inaugural lecture *Creation and Environment*[33] maintains that only an approach which affirms the ontological continuity between creator and creation can overcome what he sees as the devastating effects of a transcendentalist theology on the environment. The terms he uses to describe the contrasting approaches are the 'organic' versus the 'monarchical' models of God. He traces the monarchical view back to attempts in the Middle Ages to reject natural theology and to derive creation from the will of God rather than from his nature. The line of succession (or regression) he traces from Occam, Duns Scotus, Calvin, Barth, Gogarten and Brunner to the secular theologians, concluding:

> I believe that for the majority the doctrine of voluntary creation has led to depriving the world of intrinsic interest and to seeing it primarily in a utilitarian way as an object for exploitation.[34]

Macquarrie's thesis is, I think, open to question at a

number of points. It is clear, for instance, that the monarchical view of God was no mediaeval invention, and while
voluntarism as a self-conscious theological category may
have been, an understanding of the primacy of God's will
was established long before then. In the Old Testament the
most characteristic picture of God was that of a monarch who
laid down his own terms for initiating covenant relationship
with his people, and that informed their view of his creating
at the beginning by the power of his word. In the New
Testament that picture is far from obliterated, and Jesus
who called God 'Abba' just as often used metaphors of king
and kingdom and did not set the one against the other. The
causal link which Macquarrie sees between voluntarist-
monarchical and exploitative is just as hard to maintain, and
Tillich dismisses as meaningless[35] the distinction between
creation as necessary or as contingent act of God, a distinction which is at the heart of Macquarrie's argument.

These points aside, it is still worth asking whether the
organic model, or ontological approach as I have called it,
does give a better basis for ecological responsibility than the
monarchical or transcendentalist one. Certainly if Tillich's
writing is taken as an example of the organic model there are
grounds here on which a theology for the care of the environment can be built.[36] Within his view of 'originating creativity', for example, there is a reaffirmation of the goodness and
worth of the entire creation, the material included. 'God as
creator is equally near the material and the spiritual',[37] and
there is no justification for human arrogance toward other
creatures, for while the distinction between them is an
ontological one, this does not imply a difference in value.
In fact the non-human can be perfect in a way that the
human is not for only the latter is free to disobey. This
capacity that the human creature has for self-actualization
in freedom has both positive and negative implications for
living in the context of environmental crisis. Positively, it
makes possible real transformation of human lives and

attitudes and consequently new hope for the world through genuine* human creativity. Negatively, it brings the threat of further estrangement and distortion of human capabilities, and consequently the destruction of the natural order. This negative possibility is explored further in Tillich's view of the fall, and there again is guidance for the ecologically concerned, for while the depth of human sinfulness is not denied, the necessity of environmental catastrophe is. By denying an actual pre-fallen state Tillich discredits futile attempts to escape responsible action, either by trying to reproduce an original environment of the innocence of nature, or by retreating into inertia brought on by the despairing conviction that fallen man is bound to destroy the world. Tillich's view makes it clear on the one hand that no perfect state of nature can exist because the whole of creation is, like man, living under the conditions of existence, and on the other that while humans add to the deterioration of the environment, its destruction is not inevitable. His view of new creation is similarly inclusive, understanding as he does that

> essentialization or elevation of the positive into Eternal Life [is] a matter of universal participation: in the essence of the least actualized individual, the essences of other individuals and, indirectly, of all beings are present . . . Eternal blessedness is also attributed to those who participate in the Divine Life, not to man only, but to everything that is. The symbol of a 'new heaven and a new earth' indicates the universality of the blessedness of the fulfilled Kingdom of God.[38]

On this reading of Tillich I would agree with Macquarrie that the organic model can provide a sound theological basis for ecological concern. However, I do not agree that the monarchical cannot. True, some who believe that God's creative act was an exercise of free sovereign will rather than a necessary outgrowth of his nature have condoned exploitation of the natural world, but this attitude does not follow necessarily from a monarchical-voluntarist view. Why should the idea of a world created by the free grace of the sovereign Lord and given man for his responsible use lead to a lack of interest or to exploitation? There is no evidence that Jews who held to the monarchical model were any more exploiters of the natural world than Christians influenced by the Greek philosophical view that Macquarrie commends. Luther, whom Macquarrie excuses from the black list of other Reformers because of his praise for the work of God in creation, was just as much a voluntarist as the others and retained an uncompromisingly monarchical view of God. There are, it seems to me, no logical, philosophical or theological grounds for losing interest in the world, as Macquarrie suggests, when it is seen as other than, rather than as extension of, the being of God. Why should a world that God chose to create have less intrinsic value than one he had to bring into being? It could be argued just as strongly that a world created by God's gracious choice, given to people to live in and to care for, gains in appeal over a world brought into being and peopled so that God could give expression to his own nature. In any case there are clearly grounds within the monarchical approach for taking the world just as seriously as in the organic model, for living within it joyfully, and for acting responsibly for its preservation and renewal.

7. Existentialist: Rudolf Bultmann

The label 'existentialist' has been applied so widely, to everything from art forms to life styles, from women's fashions to musical rhythms, from architectural designs to philosophical theories, and with such varied readings on the applause-meter, that some further clarification is needed before it can be applied to the themes under consideration.

1. *Starting-point: The Concentration on Human Existence*

In the context of theology, it is best to reserve the term 'existentialist' for those approaches to doctrine that share four main features.

First, the view that only those statements are meaningful that say something to human existence. This is not to claim that meaningful statements must refer to human existence and nothing else, although some existentialist philosophers may insist on that.[1] It is to say that no doctrinal statements are to be left so much up in the air that they say nothing to human existence. When they refer to God, therefore, they must also address human self-understanding, and where biblical or theological affirmations do not appear to do this they must be interpreted so that they do. Otherwise, as Bultmann put it, those making the statements repeat the sin of Adam because they try to examine God and to discuss his ways without putting themselves under scrutiny.[2]

Second, it is not enough that the references to human existence should be in general terms. To be genuinely existential they must address one's own existence in the present. The doctrine must say something about how I am to understand myself, how I am to decide, to respond, to act in my own situation in the present. So, for instance, the assertion 'God is immortal' must be seen to have the corollary 'man is mortal' so that man too is addressed; but more than that, it gains existential significance only when one feels the force of the further implication 'one day I must die', or even, 'I may die today'.

Third, the self thus addressed is seen primarily in historical rather than natural terms. This does not mean that the emphasis is on the past. On the contrary, emphasis is put on present existence, but this present existence is seen to be constituted in historical decisions. In other words, what makes us what we are is not some essential nature built in from the beginning and inexorably developing into what we now are, but the successive decisions that we have made throughout our lives that have shaped what we have become. 'Invent the sort of self you are to be, and stick to your invention' was the advice Sartre is said to have given to a disillusioned young soldier whose life had lost all meaning. According to the existentialist, therefore, there is a real sense in which we do make ourselves. We are the product of what has happened to us and the way we have responded.

Fourth, closely related to this, the historicity of the self becomes the primary dimension of history. Nature as the objective realm of 'natural phenomena' (the cycle of seasons, the life of animals, and so on), and history as the past history of people and of nations, are existentially insignificant until they impinge upon a person's existence in the present, and only then do they become constitutive of his history. Therefore, to say that humans are historical beings is not just to acknowledge that existence is bound up with the course of world history. It is also to recognize that existence is made up within the framework of decisions taken in the present by which 'the yield of the past is gathered in and the meaning of the future is chosen'.[3]

Taking Bultmann who has consistently championed the cause of an existential hermeneutic as the typical exponent of this approach, how are the themes of creation, fall and new creation then understood?

2. *Creation and Self-understanding*

> Only such statements about God are legitimate as express the existential relation between God and man. Statements which speak of God's actions as cosmic events are illegitimate. The affirmation that God is creator cannot be a theoretical statement about God as *creator mundi* in a general sense. The affirmation can only be a personal confession that I understand myself to be a creature which owes its existence to God.[4]

According to the existentialist view, therefore, the doctrine of creation refers to the historicity of man rather than to the origin of the cosmos. It is not a theory about the past but an affirmation about the present that shows man how he is to understand himself. Faith in creation, Bultmann insists, 'is the expression of a specific understanding of human existence'.[5]

But what is this specific understanding conveyed by the doctrine of creation? It is possible to answer that in a way that reflects both the spirit and letter of Bultmann's views, for in the nineteen-thirties he preached two sermons explicitly on that subject, and they both arose out of the situation in Germany at that time when the Church had to face the reality and the implications of the Nazi rise to power. This posed in an acute form the question of how to live in the world, participating in the life of the nation on the one hand, yet not worshipping the worldly powers on the other. No longer merely in theory but now in pressing terms of obedience and disobedience, life and death, Bultmann faced with his fellow Christians the issue of how to take the doctrine of creation seriously while retaining the centrality of the Christ-event.

One of these sermons[6] was about Paul's answer to the Corinthians' question of whether Christians could eat meat that had been offered to idols. In a way the answer seemed obvious. The idols were not really gods, so why not? Nothing had happened to the meat, so whether they ate or not was a matter of indifference. But to eat did run the danger of appearing to participate in pagan sacrifice and thus to endorse the underlying pagan beliefs. Not only would that be a bad example; it could also *give* power to the 'no-gods' by allowing belief in them to influence the way we act. To work this out in the context of Nazi Germany: of course Christians must be free to participate in the world and to take their part in building the nation. This is, after all, God's world, and human life and the life of the nations come from him. Yet to participate may also have the effect of giving undue authority to the worldly powers, condoning unquestioning obedience to, and adulation of, nation, race and Führer, giving to the no-gods power that belongs to God alone.

Into this comes the Pauline proclamation of God as creator. 'For us there is one God from whom are all things and for whom we exist.' Therefore all other beings and all other powers that pose as divine are in themselves nothing. The best way of coming to an existential interpretation of that reference is to see what Bultmann himself had to say:

If we really want to grasp what Paul means, we must not get hung up on the images in which ancient thought tried to make human existence understandable, but rather must reflect on the actualities that are intended in such images. Certainly for us the images of bands of demons and divine figures have to come to an end. But have the powers also come to an end whose efficacy and claim once found expression in these images? By no means!

. . . modern man's idol . . . is the vital power that is at work in natural life and gives form to the *nomos* of nation and state . . . Wherever the ultimate reality that gives

meaning to our life and demands our worship is seen to
lie in these powers, the many gods and lords still hold
sway . . . But Paul says of all these powers that they are
nothing in the face of the one and only God . . .

Thus the first thing that is expressed by the Christian
idea of God as the Creator is that *God stands beyond all the
great powers of nature and history and of national and spiritual
life,* in whose realm we exist, who lay claim to us and . . .
demand our devotion. Here, in *this* realm, God is not to
be found! If we serve these powers we do not yet thereby
serve God: if we give them the glory we refuse it to God
the Creator.[7]

To have faith in God as creator, then, is to be aware of the
nothingness of the world and of its powers. It is also to
realize that we are encompassed by the same nothingness. To
affirm that we are created *ex nihilo* is not to talk about the
origins of the human race but about our present existence.
We are still nothing in ourselves. We are, and continue to
be, only in relationship to our creator, and our whole life
is set within these creaturely limits.

Legend[8] has it that Philip of Macedonia gave orders that
every day he should be wakened by a servant who shouted:
'King Philip, one day you must die!' To keep the king
humble? Yes, but also to set the stage for living each day of
his life, to mark out the boundaries within which it is to be
played out. As soon as we forget that we are in the hands of
the creator and that he alone sustains our being we begin to
be nothing.

All this, however, while of the utmost importance, is not
distinctively christian. This awareness of nothingness is
shared by the pagan who loses faith in his gods, by the
atheist who faces life without God, by the nihilist who
discovers that life has no meaning, by the hedonist who
loses his taste for pleasure, or by the Marxist whose ideology
crumbles. Such awareness becomes christian faith in creation,

Bultmann maintains, only when (and here Barthian over-tones are unmistakable) *'the second article [of the creed] stands alongside of the first.* We not only have one God, the Father, from whom are all things and for whom we exist but also *one Lord, Jesus Christ, through whom are all things and through whom we exist.'* [9]

What is the meaning of that? For the existentialist the primary reference cannot be back in the past to the beginning of cosmic chronology when the Son was said to be sharing the creative work of the Father; it must be in our own present experience, as we come to know in Jesus Christ what the creative power of God is, and, through him, become aware of the reality of new creation. Before elaborating on that, however, we need to see first how the doctrine of the fall is understood from existentialist perspective.

3. *Fallenness*

As we have seen, the existentialist approach sets out to translate doctrine from the categories of nature and past history of the world into terms of human existence in the present. An understanding of the fall must therefore begin with the experience of one's own fallenness.

When a person is faced with the kind of nothingness we have just been considering, the nothingness of the world and of himself, he experiences it as a threat and tries to secure himself against that threat. In looking at the limits of his own finitude he does not receive them with gratitude for the space and time they mark out for him to live in; he fights against them for the possibilities they exclude. But he compounds the threat by looking within the world for the weapons to fight with. He puts his trust in the derivative powers of the world, themselves limited, to set him free from the limits that go with existence in the world, but in so doing he loses the freedom he has by putting himself in bondage to these powers.

There are three aspects to this fallen or inauthentic existence.[10] First, in trying to establish ourselves securely within the world we give unwarranted power and authority to the worldly institutions, to the 'no-gods'. These powers, which have no reality of their own and no independent existence, are given authoritative status and consequently come to dominate us. Nation, race, wealth, social class, political party – once we look to any of these as the basis for our existence to which we give ultimate allegiance and from which we draw our meaning they become our masters rather than our servants. As Bultmann put it, the many gods and many lords still hold sway.

Second, when we depend so absolutely on these worldly powers we let ourselves in for the paralyzing anxiety that leads to death.[11] If we try to establish our lives on anything less than God then we are relying in an ultimate way on something that can fail and that we know can fail, and that results in *Angst*, not the useful kind of anxiety that gets the adrenalin circulating and spurs initiative and action, but the despairing and immobilizing anxiety that leaves us helpless. All the usual causes around which people rally and all the havens to which they flock can fail, and if we have put our trust unreservedly in any of these and given them our ultimate allegiance then as they show signs of failure and disintegration so do we.

Third, we are unable to extricate ourselves from this situation of fallenness. According to the existentialist, man is his history. We are what we have made of ourselves through our acts of response and responsible decision, but now we find ourselves trapped in a paradoxical situation. We are faced with the responsibility, indeed the necessity, of making decisions, and in these decisions we are actually constituting ourselves, choosing our own future and thus shaping our own existence in the present, but these decisions lose their authenticity because we are bound to our past self-understanding. In order to be free in the present and for the future the binding force of the past has to be broken. However, we are unwilling to do that, or, if willing, still unable, for that would be to get rid of ourselves. It is precisely this, to become new beings, that we are unable to achieve for ourselves.[12]

These are the terms in which Bultmann understands the universality of fallenness, not that we have inherited original sin, nor been stamped as it were with the image of Adam, but that we deliberately conform to the image of disobedient and rebellious man. We cling to what we have already, and in so doing alienate ourselves not only from our own future but also from God, because this decision for the past is at the same time an assertion of reliance on what we have made of ourselves, and that amounts to rebellion against the creator-God who gives us our being. This is a turning away from the creator toward the creation. This is to live not only in flesh (which is characteristic of every human existence as human) but according to the flesh. It is to make of the world as *kosmos* not only the 'earthly conditions of life and earthly possibilities' but also 'the implicit or explicit antithesis to the sphere of God as "the Lord" '.[13]

> As a result of his self-assertion man is a totally fallen being. He is capable of knowing that his authentic life consists in self-commitment, but he is incapable of realizing it because however hard he tries he still remains what he is, self-assertive man. So in practice authentic life becomes possible only when man is delivered from himself. It is the claim of the New Testament that this is exactly what has happened. This is precisely the meaning of that which was wrought in Christ. At the very point where man can do nothing, God steps in and acts.[14]

4. *New Creation*

It is now clear how new creation is to be understood so that it will fit the pattern of existentialist interpretation. The focal point of the doctrine of creation is to be found in human historicity. To affirm God as creator is to know that God is *my* creator and to live accordingly. This we refuse to do, until finally we are incapable of doing it. New creation is therefore God's action in doing for us what we cannot do for ourselves – he cuts us free from the bonds of the past and sets us free for a new future. 'God has acted,' Bultmann affirms, 'and the world – this world – has come to an end. Man himself has been made new.'[15]

Bultmann, despite criticism from many sides,[16] holds firmly to the New Testament proclamation that God's act of new creation is accomplished in and through Jesus Christ, but characteristically he turns attention away from the past-historical dimension, insisting that it is only in the present and for the individual who appropriates the word of salvation that Christ becomes the saving event through whom we are created anew. The past occurrence of the life and death of Jesus of Nazareth becomes the salvation-event in the present, not through any reminiscent historical account referring to what happened in the past,[17] but only through proclamation that challenges me to understand myself in terms of that event, and to act accordingly.

This approach is clearly in harmony with one main theme in the biblical witness to new creation, which is that this occurs here and now in the life of the faithful who are in Christ. 'When anyone is united to Christ, there is a new act of creation' (2 Cor. 5:17). But what of the expectation for the future and for the whole of the rest of creation? The existentialist takes account of these, but not as different themes. They are interpreted as different aspects of, or different ways of speaking symbolically about, the event already referred to, the salvation-event that occurs in personal history in the present. This way of interpreting the biblical witness is reflected in Bultmann's consistent use of the term 'eschatological event' for this saving act of God, the event of new creation which occurs in the present experience of one who is in Christ. As the following passages show, the expectations both for the future and for the world are translated into terms of present experience in the believer's own history:

> According to the New Testament, Jesus Christ is the eschatological event, which means that he is the action of God by which he has set an end to the old world. In the preaching of the Christian Church the eschatological event will ever again become present and becomes present ever again in faith. The old world has reached its end for the believer. He is a new creation in Christ. For the old world has reached its end for him in so far as he himself as the old man has reached his end and is now a new man, a free man.[18]

> Thus eschatological existence has become possible. God has acted and the world – this world – has come to an end. Man himself has been made new.[19]

Here, as we can see, a relation has been retained between beginning and end, creation and new creation, but whereas the biblical writers projected from their present experience back to the beginning and on to the end, Bultmann uses past and future but projects them as dimensions of present self-understanding.

5. *Evaluation*

It is just this shift in emphasis away from the past and future of nature and the world to human existence, personal and present, that has been most widely and consistently criticized, particularly in relation to Bultmann's understanding of the Christ-event. The arguments about the weakness of the link between past occurrence and present event, about the importance of the past objective achievement of Christ's life and about the historicity of the resurrection have been thoroughly canvassed elsewhere. Our project leads us to concentrate on what Bultmann claims the eschatological event achieves – eschatological existence, the life into which we are created anew by God's act in Jesus Christ. In particular we need to ask about the effects of concentrating on history virtually to the exclusion of nature, and on personal history rather than world history. Does this remove the realm of nature, and our lives as natural creatures, from theological consideration? Does re-creation of the self have nothing to do with the renewal of the natural order? Is the history of the nations to be relegated to an incidental back-drop to the all-important drama of the individual life? Does this isolate personal salvation from the restoration of society? Is social ethics dwarfed by the magnification of personal ethics?

(a) *Eschatological existence and world history.* Bultmann certainly seems to downgrade the importance of our involvement in the life of society and nation, even to the point of equating new creation with renunciation of the world. He tells the man who can find no meaning in life not to look around into the affairs of men and nations but into his own personal history; only there can the pattern of meaning be realized.[20] The major features of eschatological existence Bultmann identifies as 'freedom from the world', 'withdrawal from the world' or 'detachment from the world',[21] being 'taken out of the world',[22] and 'dealing with the world as if it were not'.[23] Some have seen a connection between this typically existentialist view of the life of faith and the fact that Bultmann, although himself a member of the Confessing Church, still preached a great many sermons between 1935 and 1945 that seem strangely remote from all the turmoil of the time.[24]

However, while in terms of pages written and words preached Bultmann may have given scant coverage to the social and political arena, it is not true to say that his approach necessarily leads to a denial of its importance. On the contrary, undeveloped though it may be in Bultmann's own writing, this approach does provide a clearly-defined perspective from which to view world history and does lay down terms for our involvement in it. We begin to recognize this when we see that Bultmann, following Paul, sees the world in two senses – as the complex of things and occurrences which form the necessary context for human life, and the same complex which comes to enslave people when they try to find security solely within it. To say that the believer is taken out of the world by God's saving act is to say that he is released from the bondage of the world in the second sense, not that he is excused from responsibility within the first. So, withdrawal from the world which is a feature of having been created anew means a reversal of the decision for the creation rather than the creator. It means a break with past self-understanding and the restoration of free decision by which one's own history may be renewed. This gives no immunity from responsibility within the world; it gives freedom for decision in direct response to God who is encountered in the world.

It is this understanding of detachment from the world that provides the basis for an ethic of radical obedience. Being withdrawn from the world means being free from having to accept the world's standards for judging right and wrong. It means being free from formal authority and from the binding force of ethical theories that lay down rules for action prior to the event. It means being free for a decision in which people stand in the present before the demand of God and in which their whole being is at stake. It is not being free from the demands of the world because it is precisely through these that we encounter the call to be obedient to God:

> Renunciation of the world represents no escapism or asceticism, but an otherworldliness which is simply being ready for God's command, summoning men to abandon all earthly ties. On the positive side and complementary to it is the commandment of love, in which a man turns

away from self and places himself at the disposal of others. In doing this, he has decided for God.[25]

Although the newly created being is no longer bound to the world as he was in the past, nevertheless the future for which he is now free is still a future within history, and Bultmann insists that it is just his detachment from the world that enables the man of faith to live in the world obedient to God and in love for neighbour. It is just because he knows that his destiny is not finally determined by the world and its structures that he is able to live creatively within these, speaking critically and acting for reform when necessary. It is just because he knows that the meaning of this world does not derive from itself but from its creator that man can face the apparent absurdities of the world and still take it seriously enough to live within it.

This approach makes it possible to affirm the positive value of the social and political structures of the world, at the same time reserving a basis from which to attack any attempt to make them ultimate. It is worth remembering that Bultmann's two sermons on creation referred to above were at the same time answers to the question, 'How far can christian allegiance to the state go?' The answer in each was the same – christian faith in God as creator demands that our participation in and use of the worldly powers is always limited. It depends on 'our becoming clear ourselves and also seeing that no misunderstanding arises in the minds of others, that for us these powers are not ultimate powers, that beyond them stands the creative power of God that forbids us to fall down and worship them because all glory belongs to him as the Creator'.[26]

These were significant and courageous words that needed to be heard in Germany in the nineteen-thirties. They also need to be heard again when government and government agencies in what we call democratic as well as totalitarian countries demand allegiance of a kind that over-rules all other commitments and standards for moral action, and that provides for no effective means of reservation or dissent. It needs to be heard also when secular theologies or theologies of revolution are easily distorted so that they compound the same error, of identifying particular movements unambiguously as God's work in the world, demanding uncritical commitment to them. This is not to say that God cannot be at work within these, nor to say that Christians should steer clear of all such movements because they will necessarily be less than perfect. It is to insist that belief in God as creator always has these two implications – it shows us the value of human life and points to the world as the context within which we live the life God gives us; at the same time it sets limits to the authority of every worldly institution, freeing us to give absolute allegiance to God alone and opening our eyes to see that this allegiance is fulfilled only in love for others.

(b) *Nature and new creation.* Bultmann draws a sharp distinction between nature and history. As early as 1926 he was contending that our relationship to history is wholly different from our relationship to nature:

> Man, if he rightly understands himself, differentiates himself from nature. When he observes nature, he perceives there something objective which is not himself. When he turns his attention to history, however, he must admit himself to be a part of history; he is considering a living complex of events in which he is essentially involved.[27]

Looking at that last sentence again, it seems extraordinary now to think that Bultmann failed to acknowledge that we are equally 'part of nature'. It is easy to forget that a decade ago the word 'ecology' was virtually unknown in theological discussion, but today it is hard to imagine a theologian saying that history is 'a living complex of events in which we are essentially involved' and not saying exactly the same thing about nature. Yet such a distinction appears fundamental to the existentialist approach, insisting as it does that God's acts become revelation events or saving events only as they can be appropriated as contributing to self-understanding. This occurs, so it is contended, only in history, especially in personal history as the Christ-event is appropriated and becomes decisive. Consequently it is in existential history and not in the realm of nature that God is known as creator and the source of new creation.

Not content with seeing this distinction as part of the existentialist methodology, Bultmann claimed that it was a feature of biblical thought as over against Greek philosophy. For the latter, he said, nature was the dominant category. The meaning of human life and of the world was inherent in nature and its relationships, so that the view of history was obscured and the task of historiography downgraded. In this system man became an object of investigation along with other natural objects and was important only as an individual instance of a general rule. In the biblical view, however, history is the dominant category. God reveals himself in history rather than in nature, and man finds himself and his place, not within nature as instance of general rule, but over against nature with a history given him by God.

Whatever may be said about this view of man in Greek philosophy, it is not the case that the Bible sustains that kind of sharp distinction between nature and history, as we saw in chapter 2. No doubt the prophets of Israel did call the people away from nature-gods to Yahweh whom they knew in their history, but nature was not a realm that was alien to God or to them. In the biblical witness man is seen as creature among the other creatures, depending as they did on the world of nature within which God had set them, and while man enjoyed a special place in the created order and was endowed with freedom that made history possible, being part of this history did not extract him from the realm of nature. The extension of the nature-history distinction into a division sometimes amounting to opposition[28] is a much later development, probably stemming from the Enlightenment and certainly hardening within the mould of some influential 'biblical theologies' of this century that depicted redemption solely in terms of historical drama, leaving virtually untouched the world of nature, and providing no means of celebrating salvation in terms of the care and renewal of the whole created order.

I agree with those who maintain[29] that it is then only a short step to a negative assessment of the world of nature and of that aspect of man which he shares with the rest of creation, and to the use of such assessment as a licence to act however he chooses, with no accountability toward the rest of the created order. Bultmann did not take this step, and it is not strictly accurate to attribute to him even the previous step of making an ontological separation between the realms of history and of nature, for in his later writing he says that the distinction is largely phenomenological, reflecting different methods of approach.[30] Nevertheless he was wrong to insist that the doctrine of creation is about human existence in the present *rather than* about the beginning of the world. The creation stories of Genesis, for example, proclaim the meaning of our present existence precisely by settling us firmly within the framework of nature, and to recognize their mythical character is not to require elimination of their reference to the past or to nature. Saying that humans have been set within the context of the natural world from the beginning was a graphic way of picturing the indissoluble relationship between man and the rest of the created order, and Bultmann's existential re-interpretation should not have led him to discard the references to nature, for their meaning certainly can be appropriated as part of our personal history.

Whatever the extent of the nature-history distinction that Bultmann draws, he nevertheless recognizes the responsibility that man has for the whole of the created order, and while it is, for him, in personal history that the event of new creation occurs, this is to have ramifications for the world of nature. While I agree that Bultmann overdoes the nature-history distinction and, by concentrating on personal historicity, does not take adequate account of the biblical witness to God's creation of, revelation in, and re-creative purpose for the non-human dimension of the created order, I am still more inclined to accept his view of the relation between the re-creation of man and of nature than the nature mysticism now advocated by some as a corrective to centuries of neglect. Romans 8, as Bultmann saw and as others have recently confirmed, is no 'cosmic daydream'[31] but an affirmation first of all of the new creaturehood of believers. Just as the 'fall of nature' is no blight imposed by God in retaliation for the disobedience of man but is the devastation wrought by the greed and arrogance of fallen man himself, so the renewal for which the whole creation longs will be the restoration brought about by the transformed attitude of man whom God creates anew.

8. Eschatological: Jürgen Moltmann

One of the most significant criticisms of the existentialist approach has come from Jürgen Moltmann, significant because he does not dispute the need to translate the Gospel so that it addresses the human situation in the present. Therefore when he recognizes the weaknesses in Bultmann's approach he is also able to propose a convincing alternative. This he sketched on broad canvas in the *Theology of Hope*,[1] and, having given more detailed attention to some features in essays since then,[2] has more recently added depth to the christological dimension in *The Crucified God*.

Long before Moltmann's work, and indeed before Bultmann published his demythologizing essay, Reinhold Niebuhr had anticipated a major weakness in Bultmann's proposal to remove from the Gospel the unnecessary scandal of outmoded thought-forms. Out of his experience as a pastor in Detroit, where the Church seemed incapable of coping with the opposing forces of militant unionism and implacable industry ownership that were using the lives of working people in the parish as their battleground, he wrote:

> The fact is that many more men in our modern era are irreligious because religion has failed to make civilization ethical than because it has failed to maintain an intellectual respectability. For every person who disavows religion because some ancient and universal dogma outrages his intelligence several become irreligious because the social impotence of religion outrages their conscience.[3]

For one who accepted with Bultmann the urgency of the task of translating the Gospel into thought-forms relevant to the twentieth century so that hearing and response would be possible, this relocation of the scandal hits home with peculiar force. Is there much point in proceeding with the translation project if the scandal is at the social and ethical level rather than at the biblical and theological?

Once that question is raised, Moltmann's criticism is both more radical and more constructive than the one suggested by Niebuhr. More radical because he shows that the existentialist translation itself leads to social ineffectiveness and therefore warrants rejection by modern man. More constructive because he shows how a different theological interpretation can overcome the distance between the Gospel and modern man's experience of social and political alienation.

1. *Starting-point: Hope as Theological Perspective*

Moltmann agrees that the meaning of the Gospel for the present must be rediscovered, but collapsing past and future into the present is no way to do it. That erases the most distinctive features of the Gospel and excludes the most effective way of finding present meaning. Focusing attention on individual existence is equally damaging, he maintains, and is in any case an affront to modern man who rightly scorns those who embrace hope for themselves while holding out none for the rest of humanity and the created order. It is only when the past is taken seriously, and the past history of the world and Israel in particular, not just the past history of the self, that God is recognized as a God of promise. God the creator of the world and of Israel is the one who sustains his people by giving them hope, hope which is based not on what they are capable of but on the promise of God's future action. It is just the biblical witness to God's past action in history which gives rise to hope for his action in the future, and it is just this hope for the future that makes sense of the present and gives some point to social involvement.

To put this another way. Bultmann's approach looks for

meaning within the self despite the plight of the world. New creation has already arrived within the faithful self whatever the world looks like. Moltmann's approach searches for meaning in the future action of God that makes living in the world the way it is intolerable. New creation is therefore to be made real by actions that cut across the negativities of the present. Contrast these two passages, Bultmann first:

> The man who complains: I cannot see meaning in history . . . is to be told 'Do not look around you into universal history but look into your own personal history. Always in your present lies the meaning of history . . . and you can realize it in your responsible decisions.'[4]

And Moltmann:

> Those who hope in Christ can no longer put up with reality as it is but, beginning to suffer under it, move to contradict it. Peace with God means conflict in the world because the goad of the promised future stabs into the flesh of every unfulfilled present.[5]

An integral component of this Bultmann-Moltmann contrast is their use of different categories in translating the Gospel. Bultmann uses existentialist ones, and therefore the truth-claims of christian faith are to be tested by seeing whether it is relevant to one's personal existence in the present. Moltmann uses Marxist categories and then the test is *praxis*, to see whether it provides adequate initiative for the transformation of society. If the latter test is applied, an understanding of the Gospel that does not lead to social action is not just irrelevant but is, in addition and consequently, theologically wrong. This criterion Moltmann defends on biblical grounds:

> Under the conditions of modern times the symbolism of Christian hope appears to be mythical. But it dare not dream away any longer about an eternity beyond time.

It must bring the hoped-for future into practical contact
with the misery of the present. This is necessary not only
on the basis of the modern world, it is also a demand of
Jesus himself. He not merely announced the Kingdom of
God but practised it in his love of sinners and publicans.[6]

For Moltmann, therefore, if hope is to provide an authentically theological perspective it must retain three biblical
dimensions – the action of God in the past history of Israel
which gave shape to his promises, the future action of God
which will bring the promises to fulfilment, and the present
action of man which is given direction and encouragement
by promise and hope. As we have seen, Bultmann fails because he thinks of past and future largely as aspects of the
present, and of the present of the individual. In Moltmann's
view Barth is no more successful in this respect because while
he claims that Christianity had to be 'altogether and unreservedly eschatological',[7] he deprived eschatology of its
historical co-ordinates. The eschaton was transferred from
its place as the culmination of world history to a transcen-
dental reality above history, capable of breaking into any
historical moment and therefore equidistant from every
historical event. To have an eschatology whose meaning
inheres in a suprahistorical realm distorts the biblical view
no less than one that is individualistic. What is needed,
Moltmann insists, is an eschatology that looks to the future
of the world, and in a way that consequently reshapes the
present in anticipation of what has yet to come.

2. Creation and History

Greek philosophers, in searching for a theory of being that
would satisfy the mind's concern for order and the soul's
yearning for rest and security, proposed the theses: 'What is,
is' and 'Out of nothing, nothing comes.' Over against these
Moltmann sets what he calls the ontological thesis of biblical

creation faith, 'Everything that is is created out of nothing.' To opt for the second, the dynamic rather than the static, is a risky business because it commits the believer to take his stand within the uncertainties of history, and to believe in a creator-God whose creation appears far from good and who puts himself at risk within the very history that he inaugurated.

To say that God creates out of nothing is to relinquish any guarantee of certainty or security in past or present. Creation is out of nothing, not out of some indestructible matter or eternal principle of being. Consequently no promise comes from pre-creation to ensure continuity of the world or the persistence of our own selves. No pre-existent ideal world, imperfectly mirrored by this world, stands before or behind our experience to guarantee its continuity. Creation is out of nothing and it may again become nothing. The seas were separated and the dry land formed, according to the biblical image, but the waters of chaos still threaten. Light was called out of darkness but the powers of darkness still assail us. That we are is no guarantee that we must continue to be.

> A creation out of nothingness is nevertheless simultaneously a creation within a sea of nothingness. A creation out of chaos is an order of life within chaos. Therefore creation is an open creation, open for its own destruction as well as its redemption and new creation . . . We cannot understand it therefore as the golden state of affairs before history, instead we must conceive it as the laying of the foundation and the inauguration of history. The process is inaugurated. The field of destructive and constructive possibilities is laid out.[8]

To say that God creates out of nothing is to relinquish the future as source of security as well, at least as traditionally interpreted. Christian theology and everyday piety took to themselves the myth of the eternal return[9] because it seemed to solve theological problems and meet people's needs. The theological problem of reconciling belief in a good God with an imperfect creation was solved by looking to the future reconstitution of an ideal world. The existential despair of the suffering creature was overcome by yearning for the return of the soul to the true world from which it came. If creation is out of nothing, however, there is no point in looking to the future as a return to pre-creation perfection or pre-temporal bliss. Yet there is point in looking to the future. Indeed it is only by looking to the future with hope that we are able in the present to believe in God and to live by faith. This hope, however, does not look for a return to the way things were but for God's act of new creation in which he will make all things new; an act which is prefigured by his raising Jesus from the dead in which good is brought out of evil, the godless are justified and the dead are brought to life; an act which leads us to hope against hope and to anticipate the future by embodying signs of the new creation.

Nevertheless the theodicy question is not answered by looking to the future alone, nor even by acting in the present out of hope for the future 'so that our world becomes transformed into the recognizable world of God',[10] for that can still leave us with a picture of a creator-God who, after he had laid out the field of destructive and constructive possibilities, now does nothing about the suffering brought about by the development of the destructive potentialities except to promise that all will be well at the end. Faith in the creator-God is tenable in the horror of historical suffering and the agony of repression and injustice only because the past acts of God have made him part of the suffering of his creation. An impassible God, one whose perfection allows no suffering or any kind of change, may be credible within an ontology that sees this world and its suffering as less than real and locates meaning in another realm. Once see this world as real, however, and its history as the realm in which meaning is to be found, and their creator stands condemned for uncaring neglect unless he shares their suffering.

That, Moltmann insists, is an integral part of Judeo-christian belief in God. To hold to him as creator is not to insist on his absoluteness and his freedom but to recognize that precisely because he is creator he has given up his separateness, his being with himself. To see him as creator of his people Israel is to know that he participates in their history. To believe in him as incarnate in Jesus Christ is to know that he shares the suffering of all mankind and creates a new relationship between himself and all his creatures:

> If one starts from the *pathos* of God, one does not think of God in his absoluteness and freedom, but understands his passion and his interest in terms of the history of the covenant . . . God already renounces his honour in the beginning at creation . . . Like a servant he bears Israel and its sins on his back . . . He meets men in those who are in straits, in the lowly and the small . . . [He] creates the conditions for communion with God through his self-humiliation in the death of the crucified Christ and through his exaltation of man in the resurrection of Christ . . . These *accommodations* of God to the limitations of human history at the same time contain *anticipations* of his future indwelling in his whole creation, when in the end all lands will be full of his glory.[11]

3. *The Fall as Hopelessness*

Who we are is shaped by the faith that we hold, and faith in God is possible only in the light of hope. Consequently, according to Moltmann, 'the sin of unbelief is manifestly grounded in hopelessness'.[12] In the darkness of hopelessness we tread the endless circle of the lost.

Hopelessness, Moltmann agrees,[13] can take two forms, presumption and despair, and both amount to rejection of God. They refuse to take God's promises seriously and are not prepared to wait for what he brings out of the future.

Both demand fulfilment in the present. Presumption tries to achieve it ahead of time, despair gives up expecting it at all; neither wait for God to give it. Presumption, by trying to achieve what only God can give, thereby usurps the authority of God. It is a form of self-deification which, far from making man more human or more than human, makes him less than human and more inhumane.[14] Less than human because in trying to make himself God, man loses what makes him distinctively human – the mediating role between creator and creation. More inhumane because his relation to his fellows and to the other creatures is no longer disciplined by the recognition of his own limitations and his responsibility to image God to the rest of creation. He then has unrealistic expectations for himself, makes impossible demands on others and wields unrestrained power over the rest of the created order.

And yet, says Moltmann, it is just as he realizes the boundless power in his possession that man comes up against another kind of limit, a limit which is itself as limitless as the boundary described by a circle. Once man's possibilities were severely restricted, and nature and the natural world dominated over him, but with scholarly understanding of nature and technological capacity to manipulate the natural world man came increasingly to dominate over the rest of creation. But in this situation

> man enters again a new experience of boundary... Man who rules nature via society now becomes a slave of his own products. Man's creations become autonomous, program themselves out of his control and gain the upper hand over him.[15]

It is possible to extend Moltmann's point here and to see that the boundary is once again set by the natural world, for these creations of man that now threaten to enslave him also threaten the very existence of the world in which he is enslaved. Once again man finds himself threatened by

nature, not by its dominance but by its fragility and incapacity to support him. So the vicious circles of poverty,
force and alienation in which fallen man endlessly stalks
'are now bound up in a greater circle, the *vicious circle of the
industrial pollution of nature*'.[16]

But behind and within all these circles of our fallenness
there is something more profound, 'a deeper, more embracing
drive: the *vicious circle of senselessness and godforsakenness*'.[17]
People become immobilized by the problems that face them,
fascinated and transfixed by the threats to their existence.
They are overcome by waves of purposelessness, lose all sense
of direction and even the will to struggle, no longer caring
whether they are carried along or finally submerged. This,
then, is the other aspect of the sin that is hopelessness –
double despair which gives up both on God and on ourselves
and counts not at all on the promise of new creation.

> God promises a new creation of all things in righteousness
> and peace, but man acts as if everything were as before
> and remained as before. God honours him with his
> promises, but man does not believe himself capable of
> what is required of him. That is the sin that most pro-
> foundly threatens the believer. It is not the evil he does
> but the good he does not do, not his misdeeds but his
> omissions, that accuse him. They accuse him of lack of
> hope.[18]

4. *Hope for New Creation*

Hope for the future action of God which alone makes faith
possible and answers the cry of our hopelessness is hope for
nothing less than new creation. Hope that is grounded in the
biblical witness to the God of promise is not directed to an
otherworldly escape from history or to a return to pre-
existent paradise, but to the future act of God at the end of
history. As new creation it will bring into being that which
is radically new. As new creation in Christ it finds its basis

in his death and resurrection, the bringing into being of that which was not.[19] As historical it will be oriented toward history and will encourage human involvement in history to confound present despair by anticipating the future of God.

This, however, leaves a question of major importance. It is true that hope should be for the future of the world and not just for individuals selected out of the world. It is true that hope should not allow us to rest content in the present while waiting for a better day but should create such tension between what is and what ought to be that we are driven to take action. But what action? To put this another way, Moltmann insists that the Christian lives in the context of God's promises, and his life is therefore taken up with action designed to overcome the gap between what God has promised and what remains to be fulfilled. But what has been promised?

It was difficult to find a clear answer to that in the *Theology of Hope*. In fact Moltmann tended to avoid the question by definition, almost as a matter of principle, by insisting that if the future action of God is new *creation* then we cannot know what God has in store for the world. He was fond of quoting the text, 'It does not appear what we shall be', and claimed that the resurrection of Jesus, by negating the world's judgement passed on him by the cross, shows that no human thought can anticipate the future of God. But this leaves us in a dangerous dilemma. Our hope calls us to action but does not make it clear what kind of action. We are to act anticipating the fulfilment of God's promises but cannot be sure what these promises are. Is there no way of providing more direction to the action that is fired by hope and powered by promise? A reading of the New Testament ought to find more in the death and resurrection of Jesus than the symbol of hope and of the unexpectedness of God's action. To begin with, it ought to dispel some false hopes by recalling how the hopes of many of those who knew Jesus (and might have followed him if he had issued a different kind of call to action) remained unfulfilled. The promises of God to Israel were fulfilled in a way that none of the major parties expected, nor indeed acknowledged, but from this more can be deduced than the general formula, 'God's promises are always fulfilled in an unexpected way.' It follows, for example, that God does not reserve rewards for the righteous before the law; he does not side with those who take up arms to make the chosen people a mighty nation; nor does he make his home with those who retreat into the desert in order to await the future kingdom. Consequently any hope that he will act in these ways in the future is misplaced hope, doomed to failure when translated into action.

This, I suppose, is obvious enough, but it needs to be said because Moltmann's earlier writing did seem to issue a call to action without providing sufficient criteria by which to judge its validity. Moltmann himself came to realize this, and in a recent evaluation of the theology of hope trend which he initiated he acknowledged that it 'must be made more profound if it is not to become the superficial sanctioning by religion of an officially optimistic society, sworn to economic growth and political and cultural expansion'.[20] As it happens, it has been used far more by those at the opposite end of the political spectrum, and in view of its rather doctrinaire application by some theologians of revolution Moltmann might have added, 'nor to become an indiscriminate endorsement of every movement pledged to overthrow existing economic and political structures'. Without the christological criteria which he later applied it is not surprising that Moltmann's views were taken over by theologies of revolution, and because of their continuing vogue and their link with the theology of hope it will be appropriate to take a closer look at one of these variants of the eschatological approach.

5. *Hope in Revolution*

Rubem Alves, a Brazilian who acknowledges the influence of Moltmann, re-interprets the themes of creation, fall and new creation using the political idea of revolution as the key to their understanding.[21]

(a) *God as creator.* Alves makes a great deal of the conclusion of biblical scholars that the first experience of God that Israel articulated was their experience of him in their history as the one who had made them a people. Their belief in him as creator of the world came second, Alves then maintains, not only in sequence but also in significance. The creative act of God in which he brought the people into being from nothing remained the key to Israel's self-understanding, the frame of reference within which she would interpret everything that was to happen to her and to the neighbouring nations. This primal event, Alves points out, was one in which the people were set free from slavery. Consequently God is to be understood primarily as the source of historical liberation, and humanity as the realization of historical freedom. More than that, since being human necessarily means being in community, the liberating power of God and the consequent freedom of mankind can be experienced and understood only within society. Therefore the political implications of God's acts and human response are not peripheral or optional but central and inescapable.

This creative power of God which works for human liberation is not, of course, confined to some primordial beginning nor to the inauguration of the nation Israel. God is still involved in history as its creator for he is still the source of liberation. So Alves quotes Buber with approval: 'God does not fix history from yonder side as one who is strange to it. He does not allow history to be unrolled as a scroll but he himself enters and conquers with his warfare.' Alves himself puts the point this way:

Biblical messianism is thus a different way of understanding history derived from the historical experience with the God of liberation . . . history is seen as the history of freedom, of the ongoing politics of freedom as it opens the way towards liberation.[22]

(b) *The fall.* Given this way of understanding the creative purpose of God, the fall is then seen as a symbol of the human rejection of this gift of freedom. It is a way of describing the human preference for what we have and where we are over the threatening uncertainties of what may be, and the consequent refusal to enter the future that God throws open. Since, for Alves, a biblical understanding of God as creator begins not with the first chapters of Genesis but with the saga of escape from Egypt, his paradigm for human rebellion is, predictably, the murmuring of the people in the desert rather than the defiance of Adam and Eve in the garden:

> The theological language of the community of faith was the creation of its experience with the liberating events which, together, could be described as the history of freedom. Their history, however, presented another datum: . . . the history of unfreedom. Man proved historically to be unable to live as if surfing on the waves of the political dynamics that pushes towards the future . . . Right on the journey toward the future the true voice of man is heard: rather the fleshpots of Egypt than the danger of the journey toward the promised land.[23]

Alves finds two other symbols in the Old Testament that fill out this understanding of the fall. First, the worship of Baal he interprets as another manifestation of fallenness as fear of the future. The people of Israel turned from Yahweh the God of history to worship the Baalim, gods of nature, because they found in nature the certainty of endless repetition and so an escape from the unknown future that stretched before them in history. Second, he reads the tower of Babel story in much the same way by concluding that the tower was a representative ziggurat that symbolized the linking of the earth with the heavens and thus of the people with the eternal structures of being, guaranteeing a secure place in the stable order of the universe. According to Alves, therefore, the tower story depicts human flight from the future, and since, in his view, creativity depends upon openness to the future, building the tower is a symbol not of unrestrained creativity (as I suggested in chapter 3) but its opposite – the stifling of genuine creativity. The fallen state we are in, therefore, is a state of self-assertive rebellion against God in the sense that we prefer the present situation that we can call our own to the possibilities that are given by God. This is understood in a social context, of course, and so is the sense of 'total depravity', of being trapped in this fallen state so that struggling only makes things worse. The structures of society are themselves agents of captivity that bear the marks of fallenness. Law, for instance, is not the embodiment of immutable divine values but the creation of man to serve the politics of the city of earth, and is therefore moulded by greed, pride and the will to power. The *status quo*, so often commended as orderly, peaceful and therefore good is actually a state of violence, of power directed against the new possibilities of the future. Any attempt to transform the present situation is doomed because all our blueprints for action are drawn from the models and to the scale of our present system which is programmed for its own destruction.

In *Tomorrow's Child* he works out this last point in detail, using an extended metaphor of our civilization as a dinosaur – we try to solve all our problems with the unshakable conviction that bigger is better:

> This is how the dinosaur operated. His logic was remarkably similar to that of the modern pragmatist. Both in effect keep repeating: 'I need not worry about the whole

– the whole will take care of itself.' One takes for granted the basic structure and moves on to develop its size, power and efficacy to the utmost limits. If something does not function well, it is because the system has not increased its power to the proper level at that point. Like the dinosaur, we ignore the fact that if the basic system is irrational and structurally faulty, greater power only accentuates its condition. As a strong insane man is more dangerous than a weak one, the increase of power in a sick system can only produce unexpected forms of its own derangement and eventually its downfall.[24]

(c) *New creation*. Against this background it now becomes clear that new creation can be nothing other than the creation of conditions under which human freedom is once again possible, and given this estimate of the total depravity of the existing social systems and the impossibility of renewal by modification, this must be new *creation*, i.e. the creation of something radically new. The concept of creation out of nothing is therefore taken with absolute seriousness, for out of nothing that now shapes the existing order can the new order be built. Processes of reformation, innovation and restructuring are equally impotent because all depend on oppressive institutions and distorted means of evaluation and will not be given up by those who benefit from them by any form of gentle persuasion.

How then does new creation come about? Through suffering, Alves maintains. Suffering has to be the starting-point because the dynamics of liberation can begin only when the old is negated, and that necessarily involves suffering. This view is, of course, shared by most revolutionaries and there is nothing distinctively theological about it, but Alves provides the religious dimension by affirming that God the liberator is a suffering God who suffers with and for the oppressed and persecuted. Over against humanistic messianism that depends entirely on human effort to bring about the new creation Alves proposes a messianic humanism that depends on the action of God on behalf of humanity. Humanistic messianism is mistaken, he says, because it believes that the dialectics of liberation will continue as the enslaved keep the dynamics going by continuing to protest and revolt. This, however, overlooks the clear fact of history that when the formerly enslaved gain freedom and power they in turn become oppressive and no longer keep the future open, and those who remain in bondage reach a stage of inertia if not actual contentment, preferring security to freedom. Messianic humanism, on the other hand, sees God not only suffering in and through the enslaved, but also as the one who will not allow his people to remain content with their enslavement. His suffering continues when theirs is drugged by the opiate of security:

> The history of freedom . . . cannot be based on the powers of man alone. If there is a history of freedom that negates the present and thereby creates the possibility of a new tomorrow, a history dependent on a power of freedom that transcends history and determines itself to be in and for history, it is because this power, God, does not allow the suffering of futurelessness to be dissolved into the oblivion of happiness in suffering. The slave may forget about his own suffering, but God does not. God is the suffering God, the God who does not ever allow the pains of history to be overlooked and healed by the hypnotic power of the politics of preservation.[25]

The normative biblical symbol for the suffering and liberating God Alves finds in the crucifixion and resurrection of Christ. The cross he interprets as God suffering at the hands of people who violently oppose the forces of liberation; the resurrection he sees as hope held out for the final victory of the liberators.[26]

Alves' final point is that new creation occurs as God and man work together, and this he defends on the ground that it preserves the doctrines both of creation and of grace. 'In the context of God's politics of human liberation grace creates the possibility and necessity of man's action. Man is a co-creator. The pact between God and man means that God waits for what man can give to the new tomorrow.'[27] Anticipations of this new creation are already evident in various revolutionary moves to end oppression and to liberate the captive. They are also to be seen in some aspects of the counter-culture whose members find themselves free from the demands of conformity to past-oriented mores and power-wealth-success-oriented standards. All of these, however, must be seen as no more than anticipations, as appetizers, and must not become substitutes for the fulness of the new, and for this reason Alves is highly critical of some devotees of the theology of play, the religion of experience and the liturgy of celebration. Too easily these become substitute gratifications at the individual level or within congenial self-satisfied small communities and thus destroy the resolve to work as co-creators of the fulness of what has yet to be.

I shall make some comments on this approach at the end of the next chapter. In the meantime we should note that although Moltmann's earlier writing gave some theological encouragement to the revolutionary cause, his later work has applied some significant qualifications.

6. *Revolutionary Hope*

In a number of essays written after the *Theology of Hope* Moltmann addressed himself to the question of what is implied by affirming Jesus Christ as the one in whom God's new creation becomes visible,[28] and in *The Crucified God* he set out 'to make the theology of hope more concrete, and to add the necessary power of resistance to the power of its visions to inspire to action'.[29] This he did by working out with great care and in detail what it means to see the cross of Christ as the normative action of God in the world, the action which fulfils his promise to Israel for all mankind, the action which anticipates the future action of God and the fulfilment of the new creation. God's promise is fulfilled by one who died as a blasphemer of the law, a rebel against the authorities and forsaken by God himself. Taken with radical historical serious-ness this means that the action of God towards humanity is not restricted to 'the righteous'; his grace is for the un-righteous, the powerless and the ungodly. And taken with radical theological seriousness[30] this means that in the in-carnation and crucifixion of the Son, God becomes part of the history of suffering humanity so that now nothing separates us from 'the situation of God between the grief of the Father, the love of the Son and the drive of the Spirit'.[31] Our hope lies in this, that through the cross God has made our history his history[32] and we can look forward to the final overcoming of death when sorrow will be turned into joy. Consequently action that is appropriately based on that hope will reflect the action of God in the world that he has made his own. And how do we discern the actions of God in the history of mankind? 'The criterion of perception would be the identification of God with the crucified Christ.'[33] So, Moltmann concludes, God is at work in the world wherever there are those being liberated whom Jesus lived and died to liberate, those with whom he was identified in his life and death, the poor, the oppressed, the alienated and the godless, and our actions are sacramentally joined to his as we take part in this work of liberation, setting people free from the vicious circles of economic, political, racial, cultural and ecological alienation.

But still the question remains, what *kind* of actions can have this sacramental significance? Is all action directed toward the liberation of the oppressed an 'incarnation and anticipation' of the presence of God in history? Should not the criterion of 'identification of God with the crucified Christ' be applied not only to who is to be liberated but also to how they are to be liberated, that is, in ways that are consistent with the self-giving non-resisting way of the cross?

I recognize the magnitude of the problem here, not only the difficulty of finding an answer but also the presumption of putting the question. Who am I to question how Christians in situations other than my own have decided to act? Who am I even to suggest non-retaliation to those who have been suffering, as I have not, under the organized violence of a police state? Can a simplistic distinction between means and ends be sustained in any case? Yet for all that I find the question quite inescapable, the more so since reading *The Crucified God* and seeing the question pressed by the logic of Moltmann's own argument. If the cross is to be taken, as he claims, as the action of God in and for mankind, as the starting-point for the history of the Trinity and as the normative way of God in the world, then it surely follows that this must also be the way of those whose actions are sacramentally to participate in the history of God and his re-creative work in the world.

This point will be taken up again at the end of the final chapter.

C. CONCLUSION

9. Living in the Created World

Conclusions about the biblical themes of creation, fall and new creation vary, as we have seen, with the theological perspectives that are brought to bear on them. While the last four chapters have examined, in the main, variations at the level of doctrinal formulation, each approach was seen to have its own social, political and ecological implications as well. It is in these areas that this final chapter will concentrate, looking more closely at the relationship between belief in God as creator and the life of faith and at various conclusions about how to live in the world that God has created.

I. AS ALIENS

The view that we are aliens in the world and that in order to be truly human we should as far as possible avoid involvement with, or repudiate the authority of the world, has a long and varied history.

(a) *'This earth is not our place.'* In many of the great religions the world is seen as a place where people necessarily lead an inferior existence. Its main value is to provide the means finally of escaping from the cycle of birth, death and rebirth. The life of the faithful is therefore aimed at becoming so detached from the world in this life that true life or life at one with the Absolute becomes appropriate in the next. The process of detachment may, of course, vary,[1] but there is in common the conviction that to take this world too seriously, either by acknowledging its authority wholeheartedly or by repudiating it too vehemently, is to become captive and lose one's true destiny. The mystery religions[2] also saw the world as a place of bondage, according to their view because it was under the authority of evil, the eternal forces of darkness that hold people in slavery. Appropriate action had therefore to be taken in order to escape the prison in which the powers of darkness keep us captive, namely the body. There were several main escape routes. Asceticism, by which the body could be disciplined and its demands resisted, was one. Ecstasy was another, in which the true self was allowed to 'stand outside' (*ec stasis*) through religious frenzy, the agency of drugs, or a mixture of both. Gnosis was yet another, the secret knowledge which was thought to provide more than a means of escape, for by giving the light of truth it may also convey power over the forces of darkness and lead to a genuine participation in the world now seen in its true colours.

In the world-view of the Greek philosophers the mysteries were demythologized and an alternative provided, but people were still seen to be living in an alien world. According to the Platonist view in particular, most of us know only the reality of this world and do not realize that we are aliens. Only the enlightened who have experienced the full light of Reality can know that in this world we live only with shadows and images.[3] In this world, therefore, if one cannot gain direct access to the truth by being a philosopher (which is given to few) one should then make the best of the present situation, for to achieve the good is to fulfil one's given function.

The christian view, generally speaking, runs counter to these expressions of inbuilt unreality or evil of the world, although some forms of popular piety, hymns in particular, reflect similar conclusions about our place in the world:

> Strangers and pilgrims here below,
> The earth, we know, is not our place;

But hasten through the vale of woe,
And, restless to behold Thy face,
Swift to our heavenly country move,
Our everlasting home above. (Charles Wesley)

Against this, the main weight of biblical witness affirms, as
we have seen, that this world is God's creation and is therefore good. Since life in this world is God's gift then in this
world is to be found our destiny. God is known not by escaping from or hurrying through the world but within events in
history in which he acts and makes himself known. The
alienation that does occur is not due simply to our being in
the world but to our rebellion, not to our being creatures but
to our self-assertive creativity (cf. chapter 3, section 4 above).
It is because of this rebellion that life is hard, that we are
alienated from our fellows, from other creatures and from
much of the beauty, order and fruitfulness of the world. The
overcoming of alienation is therefore seen largely in terms of
the transformation of this world, not escaping from the world
but fulfilling its possibilities. Old Testament expectation is
related to the life and hope of the nation, and the final consummation is set in this-worldly context. The New Testament
proclaims the fulfilment of Old Testament expectation in in
carnation, enfleshment of divine reality which was nonsense
according to the Greek view. Images of the consummation include (although they go beyond) the restoration of the
harmony of the created order. The heavenly city comes to
earth, the Son of Man returns, God's dwelling-place is with
men.

Faced with the threat of absorption of christian faith into
the dualism of Greek philosophy and of Gnosticism, the early
Church deliberately repudiated those views that denied the
reality or worth of this world. Marcionism, which tried to
stress the radical newness of the faith and consequently its
discontinuity with the past, was rejected because it did not
identify God the creator of the world with God its saviour.

Gnosticism, which counselled disengagement from the world and claimed salvation for the soul but not the body, was attacked by Irenaeus as *blasphemia creatoris*, blasphemy of creation.

(b) *Christian faith and alienation*. There is, however, one characteristic way of interpreting the Gospel which, while not endorsing the kind of dualism we have been looking at, nevertheless sees man as an alien in the world. The man of faith who is saved thereby becomes, it is claimed, an alien in a still fallen world. Some individuals may be created anew, but not all, and certainly not the community as a whole nor the society of nations.

If the doctrine of the fall is given a dominant place and taken to mean that since man's rebellion the whole world is under Satan's power, or that the world and the worldly authorities are depraved and corrupt, then although the world as God's creation may originally have been good, now it is evil. It can be seen as good only in anticipation of its restoration in the last days. In the meantime the Christian must live as an alien in an otherwise sinful world. His participation in society and its structures will be minimal in order to lessen the danger of infection from the world, perhaps living in a community of the saved whose organization will attempt to mirror the kingdom of God and anticipate its coming fulfilment. He recognizes the authority of worldly institutions only provisionally, fulfilling the demands of state and nation, for example, only as they coincide with what he believes to be the demands of God. Throughout the history of the Church there have been people who have taken this view, citing particular New Testament verses and the contrast drawn in some passages between loving the world and loving God, or between being bound to 'this world' and living the life for which Christ sets us free.[4] They have concluded that to live as citizens of heaven means to give allegiance to God alone and have recognized as authoritative only those institutions that stand over against the world. This could be illustrated by listing the most important representatives from the first century to the twentieth, but more light may be shed by discussing in a little more detail one from the early Church, and then suggesting some contemporary parallels.

(c) *Tertullian*, who lived and wrote toward the end of the second century and the beginning of the third,[5] when no Christian could escape the question of his relation to Roman civilization, insisted that loyalty to God demanded the rejection of the world and its institutions, and by 'world' here he meant not nature but culture, not the good creation of God but the evil result of the rebellious exercise of human creativity. This rejection was parallel to his rejection of reason as the path to true knowledge of God and his call to follow the way of faith.[6]

At the basis of this was his emphasis on the fall and its consequences. He did not deny that the universe and the soul are by nature good, for they were created by God. Yet, he insists, 'we must not consider by whom things were *made* but by whom they have been perverted . . . between the created and the corrupted state there is a vast difference'.[7] Against the view that new creation is the power that humanizes man and whose influence made civilization possible he affirmed that 'Christ came not to bring savages . . . into some civilization . . . but as one who aimed to enlighten men already civilized, and under the illusion from their very culture, that they might come to the knowledge of the truth'.[8] There is no suggestion here that the worldly institutions might be accepted, much less commended or supported as agencies of new creation. In this present age only the life of individuals may show God's recreative power overcoming the effects of the fall.[9]

How then is the Christian to live in the world? I recently heard a Hungarian's answer to that, in which he concluded:

'We Christians are not looked on as very good citizens. We are not seen to support the state with much enthusiasm.' Applied to Tertullian and those who went along with him that would have been a model of understatement. They gave political life a wide berth because they saw a basic contradiction between christian faith and the institutions of pagan culture. To become involved in the political scene was to put oneself under the authority of the opponents of God's kingdom and those who denied the new creation seen in Jesus Christ. Military service could not be undertaken either, because it required an oath of allegiance, putting the soldier under the authority of one who falsely claimed the status that belongs to God alone.[10] More, it directly contravenes the will of Christ that prohibits killing. Although in theory the same strictures do not apply against being a civil servant, in practice to support the state's provision of law and order by participating in the judiciary would involve compromise and must therefore be rejected. Granted the theoretical possibility of remaining obedient to Christ while holding state office, face the fact, said Tertullian, that the position is really untenable:

> Never sacrifice, never authorize a sacrifice, never contract for sacrificial victims, never delegate the supervision of a temple, never handle their taxes, never give a show at his own expense or the State's, never preside over one, never announce or order a festival, never even take an oath; and on top of all that, in the exercise of his magisterial authority, never try anyone on a capital charge or one involving loss of civil status, never condemn to death by verdict or legislation, never put a man in irons or in prison, never put to torture . . . [then] he may hold his office![11]

Yet Tertullian refused to align himself with those who wanted to withdraw from life in the world seen as such to be evil. 'We are not Brahmans, naked sages of India, dwellers in forests, exiles from life', he said to the Romans 'We reject.

no fruit of God's labours. Not without your forum, your meat-market, your baths, shops, factories, inns, market-days and all kinds of business, we live together with you in this world.'[12] In the face of that it is difficult to refute the charge that this is the attitude of a parasite, contributing nothing to the protection and order of the state while profiting from both, a charge commonly made in our own time against conscientious objectors to military service who cite grounds much like those of Tertullian centuries ago. Tertullian contended, however, that Christians were neither enemies of nor parasites on the state, but were true patriots because they were doing what was really needed for the true life and health of the Empire rather than conforming to false hopes for its preservation. By refusing to acknowledge the ultimacy of the state they did not threaten its life but helped to save it from the judgement of God who stays his hand against the idolatrous majority for the sake of the righteous few. And by praying not to the Emperor, which is worse than useless, but to God *for* the Emperor, Christians are among the few who take effective action to preserve the state. Other attempts are based on a lie and are therefore doomed to failure.

(d) *In our own time* there are many examples of similar conclusions about living in the world. In addition to some Orthodox and Catholic monastic communities and Protestant groups whose present way of life continues a pattern of withdrawal or seclusion set for centuries, recent decades have seen the rise of others whose antecedents are not so clear. We may have to go back two thousand years to find the inspiration for some current spiritualist and theosophist groups whose members claim, as the Gnostics did, specially conveyed insight into the unreality of this world and the reality of the true world that lies behind or beyond it. In the case of one group whose centre is in the hills on the outskirts of Melbourne,[13] this seems to owe as much to neo-Platonism and to Buddhism as to Christianity, with a tendency to downgrade the body and this world, commending withdrawal from worldly responsibility and living in close contact with other initiates who, through mystical contemplation, seek ecstatic vision and insight into reality.

There have been many other individuals, and groups with greater or less organization, that have been equally convinced of the need to live as aliens in a fallen world that is hopelessly enmeshed in evil and headed for destruction. Characteristic of such groups in the Western world is the conviction that society demands conformity to an attitude, outlook, set of values or way of life that is so perverted that it is beyond transformation from within. It must be repudiated by living a life with a radically different orientation, and that can be done only by living in a community organized around a radically different principle – the ethical standards of the new order. Disengagement is therefore essential, perhaps for the ultimate good of society but certainly for one's own sake in order to become genuinely human, or, in the explicitly christian versions of this attitude, in order to become and to remain a member of the Kingdom. Some hope to influence the rest of society by their action, by returning to nature to give an example of renewing the good earth, or, by setting up ideal relationships, to witness to Jesus as the only source and possibility of true community, but this is to be distinguished from 'the old liberal preoccupation of trying to make a sick world well'.[14] Instead, as one spokesman put it, 'we're called to *act well* by the power of Christ'. The first priority is to live by the ethics of the kingdom of God rather than by the ways of the kingdoms of this world, and that can be done only in communities that are separate and distinct from the life of the rest of society. What then happens to the rest is in the hand of God.

The kingdom perspective causes the Church-communities to see themselves as though they were colonies of settlers from another country, planted in a strange land, to bring to it the challenge of God's kingdom and his way of being accepted in it – the Gospel. They take seriously Peter's characterization of Christians as aliens and strangers here on earth.[15]

Within many local church congregations there are views which reflect the same alienist conclusion, although they do not result in the same movement into a separate community and are seldom recognized for what they are. There is, for example, the tenacious view that the church should set up organizations, societies and clubs to provide social and educational facilities so that its members will not have to become too much involved with the world outside. This was certainly the rationale, at least until very recently, for the Catholic education system in Australia which was designed, not just to provide an alternative to the state system, but to protect its children from the influence of the 'godless state schools'. In one Australian state the Methodist Church has a Department of 'Christian Tourism' for the oddly contradictory purposes of protecting Christians from the temptations encountered on secular tours, and of converting the non-Christians who go on the Church department's tours! 'Lifeline International', a grouping of counselling organizations that offer emergency services especially by telephone, was recently seriously divided over the rule that only Christians were allowed to be counsellors. In many congregations it is assumed that when church meetings clash with community responsibilities, loyalty to Christ will necessarily put church activity first. In some countries when Christians try to understand and to co-operate with non-Christians, this is denounced as a scandalous disregard of the uniquely separate place of the Christian in the world.

It is not difficult to point to inherent contradictions in many forms of this approach. Those who repudiate the rest of society still depend upon it in some way or another for their very existence, and some of the most otherworldly groups employ very worldly marketing techniques for their products. It may be important for the light of the Gospel to shine against the darkness, but how strong is the flame that has to be insulated from the chill winds of the world? Such criticism, however, too easily degenerates to the level of *ad hominem* and overlooks the fact that none of us can be free from the tension between ideal and real.[16] It is more important for our purpose to note that the more thorough-going forms of the alienist approach neglect some of the dimensions of the doctrine of creation that we have been identifying. The continuing presence of the creator-God is limited to those who acknowledge the incarnation of the Son in Jesus Christ; that he is still present to the whole of his creation and to human history is largely overlooked. The work of re-creation is seen almost exclusively in terms of the individual who is converted to Christ, and signs of the new creation within society or the wider created order are projected to the end-time. While the ethics of Jesus are taken seriously as the shape of new creation, the context of that new creation in Jesus – that it came to fulfilment within conflicting social and political forces of the world and not in isolation from them in one of the desert communities – is not. As well, while stressing the radical effects of the fall there is a failure to recognize its extent, for while the fallenness of the world is seen only too clearly, its continuing effects in whatever community of aliens is established is not. The justified sinner is a sinner still, and those who overlook that and try to organize a community of saints on earth should read again the history of monasticism, or of Calvin's theocracy in Geneva, or of Puritan settlements in New England. Not all the evil is in the world; not all the good is with the colonists of heaven.

There is, nevertheless, an important sense in which the people of faith must remain aliens. They should not feel at home in, nor content with the world as it is. Faith in God as creator, the good creator, the creator of that which is good, must lead us to see that the world is not as it should be, and to live in such a way that we are not content, and do not allow others to be content, with the world as it is. We should be alienated from the world in the way that Jesus was – not by disengaging but by refusing the world's terms for involvement, not by withdrawing but by participating on behalf of those whom the world makes alien by rejection and oppression. As Moltmann has recently put it,

> Jesus was folly to the wise, a scandal to the devout and a disturber of the peace in the eyes of the mighty. That is why he was crucified. If anyone identifies with him, this world is 'crucified' to him, as Paul said. He becomes alienated from the wisdom, religion and power politics of his society.[17]

Alienated he may be, but he does not constantly yearn for some other homeland. He is a resident alien, looking and working for the renewal of the earth given by the creator-God.[18]

2. IN COALITION

At the other end of the spectrum is the view that recognizes the world as our place where we are destined to live, and within which we should therefore feel at home. This everyday attitude may be reinforced by an understanding of creation that affirms that God made the world and sustains it by his beneficent power. The new creation in Christ is then taken to be the fulfilment of what is already present, a bridge between the old and the new that maintains a basic continuity between what now is and what God wills. Accordingly the faithful are to welcome the natural realm and human society as God-given, accepting its various cultures joyfully, and its laws as authoritative because they reflect the law of God. By endorsing and contributing to the growth of civilization we participate in the underlying driving force of the

universe which makes scientific achievement and technological advance possible, and which believers recognize as
God's continuing creative presence in the world.

(a) *The Hegelian version.* From very early in the life of the
Church, certainly from the second century and the writing
of Justin Martyr, there have been influential versions of this
approach. I take as an example a more recent representative,
both for the thorough-going attitude of his own thought and
for its impact on later theologians.

In Hegel's philosophical-theological system the idea of God
as continuous with his creation is transposed into entirely
immanentalist terms. Talk of God is translated into terms of
Absolute Spirit, and history becomes 'the unfolding of the
Absolute in time'. The continuity between the Absolute and
reality, Absolute and man, and man and the world is guaranteed by Hegel's clue to the understanding of history. What
is this clue? At first sight history appears disjointed and
chaotic, 'a vast picture of changes and transactions . . . on
every hand there is the motliest throng of events'.[19] No
pattern emerges, even when belief in Providence or progress
is brought to bear because these are too individualistic or
too vague to allow the pattern to be seen. Meaning emerges
only when three components are brought together: history
is the process of self-realization of the Spirit; this necessary
process is one of dialectical progression, of thesis-antithesis-
synthesis that reflects the same pattern of movement as
individual thought; the basic units in the historical process
are not people but states. Continuity is therefore guaranteed
– continuity between God and the world because the history
of the world *is* the unfolding of the Absolute in time; between God and man because man is part of this unfolding
process; between man and world because both are shaped
by the triadic process of Absolute Mind.

What then is man to do? Live by the truth. And Hegel
supplies the answer to Pilate's question:

Truth is the unity of the universal and subjective will. The subjective will is found in individual man, the universal is to be found in the state, in its laws, its universal and rational arrangements. The state is the actually existing moral law . . . The state is the divine idea as it exists on earth.[20]

Consequently to be genuinely human, that is, to fulfil the role that belongs to all human beings, requires the acceptance and endorsement of the authority of the state. God and state can therefore make no conflicting claims on one's loyalty because the state is the embodiment of the divine. Nor is the situation changed even when one's own state appears unjust and evil or makes unwarranted attacks on other states, because the clash then precipitated is all part of the dialectical process of contradiction and resolution within which the truth is being realized. 'My country right or wrong' is then no blind patriotism; it is a contribution to the dynamic of conflict which is the moving force of history.

Hegel's conviction that in the Germanic nations this ideal of state was being most fully embodied, when linked with the opinion that the creative presence of God was visible in the rebuilding of the nation, the reunification of the *Volk* and the strengthening of social order, lent a philosophical-theological support for the Hitler régime.

Hegel's system is an extreme form of theological immanentalism and the German christian movement was an extreme example of Church-state assimilation. That should not blind us to the regrettable fact that in her history the Church has seldom taken sides against the ruling authorities however unjust they may have become, and instances of opposition to national leaders in time of war are even fewer. Discussions of Church subservience to, or collaboration with, state usually cite well-known and widely disputed incidents and attitudes such as divine right of kings, Erastian controversies, established Churches, Vatican pacts with Fascism,

Orthodox co-existence with communism, culture-Protestant-
ism in the Bible belt, and, more recently, christian involvement in revolution and nation-building in the third world.
But many who are quite prepared to engage in learned discussions about these instances and to offer rapt attention
to plays about them often fail to recognize their own involvement in comparable trends.

(b) *Contemporary attitudes.* There is, for example, a widespread conviction that the Christian has an overwhelming
responsibility to be patriotic, to accept the authority of the
state and to abide by the laws of the land. That may be fair
enough, but when there is a conflict of authorities leading to a
crisis of conscience, the conscience that does not go along
with the claims of the state is usually judged defective.
Especially in times of actual or contrived emergency, patriotism is identified with endorsing government policy and is en-
shrined as the highest of christian virtues. Even when people
acknowledge that the state could theoretically be so wrong
that christian opposition would be an obligation, most are
reluctant to admit that this would ever actually happen. I
became acutely aware of this in discussions held during the
Vietnam war about the conscription of National Service
trainees for active service in the war zone. When the German
Church struggle was cited as an example of christian responsibility to disobey the law, this was repeatedly dismissed
with some variant of the remark: 'How fortunate we are to
live in a country like Australia where that could never
happen.'

There is also a tendency on the local church scene to turn
Christianity into a programme for being successful in the
world without really trying to be worldly. Christian faith is
extolled as the best strategy for being a social success. People
who tithe, for instance, sometimes testify to its benefits
by claiming that since they began to tithe their business has
never looked back. The Gospel is proclaimed as a form of

positive thinking that gives peace of mind and consequent success in life's everyday struggles. The idea that being a good citizen and being a church member go hand in hand is extended to imply that holding to the faith will never demand anything of us that interferes with our standing on the social ladder. No discontinuity is permitted between the demands of Church and society.

With rather more theological self-consciousness some versions of the liberal theologies of the nineteenth and twentieth centuries, and the secular and death-of-God movements of the nineteen-sixties, followed the policy of coalition. The liberals,[21] despite wide variation in views, held in common that there was no discontinuity between what was being discovered and achieved by scientific expertise, and christian faith. There was therefore no need for Christians to assert the authority of the Church or of the creeds in order to meet imagined threats from science and technology. History, for example, pursued with scientific and critical objectivity, discovers in the Gospels a historical Jesus worthy of the title 'Lord'. Biology is simply the informed way of discovering how the creator has ordered the life forms of the universe. The progress and spread of civilization being achieved through technology and politics is nothing other than God's new creation in process of realization.

In the nineteen-sixties, despite the pounding given liberal optimism by two world wars, world-wide depression, the cold war, Hiroshima and Nagasaki, Korea and Vietnam, the failures of the great society, the new society and the just society, there developed in the USA another version of this approach. It began with the secularization formula that man must find himself and his destiny entirely in secular responsibility within the world. It was extended through the conviction that to believe in God as creator and in man as given freedom by God is to conclude that the world has been handed over to man who must now live with no appeal for intervention from a transcendent God. It reached its extreme form in the 'death-of-God' theology, especially of William Hamilton who maintained that people are released to be genuinely human only by affirming the death of God. Faith and culture come together in this, that the validity of any theology is to be gauged by the extent to which it catches and reflects the mood and attitudes of the culture for which it was intended. Neo-orthodoxy with its pessimistic view of man was no longer appropriate to the optimism of American society of the nineteen-sixties. Death of theology, according to Hamilton, was.

> I think that the new optimism is both a cause and a consequence of the basic theological experience which we today call the death of God . . . This is not an optimism of grace but a worldly optimism I am defending. It faces despair not with the conviction that out of it God can bring hope but with the conviction that the human conditions that created it can be overcome . . . If I have seen this mood at all accurately then we might be able to conclude that tragedy is culturally impossible or unlikely. We trust the world, we trust the future . . .[22]

Events were very quickly to show just how wide of the mark Hamilton's estimate of the mood of America was, and if, as he maintained, matching the cultural mood is the test of a valid theology, his views must score an all-time low.

Other variations of this approach, however, cannot be written off so quickly. They do understand the doctrine of creation in such a way that the continuing power of God in the world is recognized, and our call to respond to his creative presence stressed. The significance of this life and of the world are emphasized. This life is seen as important in itself and not just as a proving-ground for a future life, and this gives a basis for genuine and not self-interested concern for others and for the society in which they live. Impetus is therefore provided for movements of reform, and positive value is given to religious and cultural achievements outside the narrow range of christian faith.

There are, however, serious limitations. By neglecting the doctrine of the fall there is a tendency over-enthusiastically to endorse all political and cultural developments, making it difficult to find a basis for critical evaluation, discrimination and judgement. This tendency is sometimes exaggerated by a view of incarnation that suggests that God 'took all of human nature as it was, put his seal of approval on it and therefore ratified nature as revelation',[23] neglecting the fact that by being incarnate uniquely in Jesus, God 'broke through the borders of man's definition of what is human and gave a new formative definition'.[24] Then the tragic dimension in life, its irrationalities and enigmas, are over-looked, superficial estimates of the problems of society are consequently offered, and unrealistic solutions propounded.

This approach, Niebuhr maintained, is based on two fallacious beliefs – the inevitability of progress and the perfectibility of human nature. Another approach to the doctrines of creation and new creation is needed to correct the first, and another look at the doctrine of the fall for the second.

3. AS INNOVATORS

Jürgen Moltmann is fond of quoting these two sentences from Rauschenbusch: 'Ascetic Christianity called the world evil and left it. Humanity is waiting for a revolutionary Christianity that will call the world evil and change it.'[25] If christian hope includes belief that here and now our guilt is cancelled, that already we are declared righteous and begin to live the new life of the Kingdom, why should we not expect and begin to live out the other features of the anticipated kingdom of God – a new humanity, a new earth? We expect to show signs of the new creation in our own lives, not just by waiting to be transformed but by living as those who are transformed. Should we not also expect some signs of a transformed society, not just by waiting for them to appear but by taking action so that they will?

This is the point at which living as aliens and in coalition intersect, despite diametrically opposed evaluations of society to begin with. One sees it as fallen and therefore to be shunned, the other sees it as the creative presence of God in the world and therefore to be endorsed. Both, however, leave it without grounds for a radical transformation, for one says it is not worth it while the other claims it does no need it.

Is there an approach that recognizes both that the world is God's good creation and that the fall is to be taken seriously, an approach that recognizes both that this fallen world is our home and that society is to be transformed and not merely endorsed? H. Richard Niebuhr, under the heading of 'Christ the transformer of culture', suggested that there is and went on to describe some of the possibilities. A number of otherwise disparate theologies seem to converge at this point,[26] suggesting an approach that does have biblical warrant and can provide a basis for faithful involvement in contemporary society. What emerges is something like the following.

(a) *Creation, fall and new creation.* Biblical witness to God as creator, it must be recognized, and to Jesus Christ as the one in whom this creative work is manifest, is set within the world-view of the time. This saw the world as surrounded with, and profoundly influenced by mysterious and threatening supernatural powers, the elemental forces of the universe; this, despite an increasing fascination among some for astrology and the occult, is not the way we see the world. Is there any point then in continuing to think in terms of the cosmic powers that Christ faced and overcame through his life and death and resurrection, making them subject and inaugurating the new creation? To ask Bultmann's question

once again: 'For us the images of bands of demons and divine
figures have come to an end. But have the powers also come
to an end whose efficacy and claim once found expression in
these images?'[27] His answer was, 'By no means', and I am
sure he is right.

We are certainly surrounded by powers and authorities,
by forces, structures and organizations that shape our lives,
give them form and reality, and in large measure make us
what we are. They may not be supernatural, but they are
supra-personal, larger than any individual, and have their
effect upon us whether we like it or not. They may be identified in different ways, and John Yoder[28] suggests a useful
grouping under five headings – the political powers of
nation, state and government; the social powers, of family,
race and class; the intellectual, which he calls the 'ologies'
and the 'isms'; the moral authorities, codes, customs and
conventions; and, of course, the religious powers, beliefs,
organizations, denominations and hierarchy. All of these
and many more are the powers or authorities (*exousia*) which
have profound influence and may come to dominate our lives.

To believe in God as creator is to believe, in the first place,
that these powers are given by God as part of his creation –
not that he fashioned these along with the stars and the sun
and the dry land, but that as one who is still creator he
brings our lives into being and fruition within the context of
these powers. Part of being human is to live within these
structures which provide a regulated network of relationships
and therefore enable us to live meaningful and enjoyable
lives; lives, that is, which are created (orderly) rather than
chaotic. However, to take the doctrine of the fall seriously is
to recognize, as van den Heuvel puts it, that these powers
are two-faced. Created to be servants they may become our
masters, not because they have that power in themselves but
because we may choose to surrender such power to them
that they finally come to enslave us. More than that, when
they do take over they change for the worse. They become

distorted, perverted, demonic. What was good as a servant becomes evil as a master. Government, for instance, becomes tyrannical; patriotism turns into fascism; faith becomes fanaticism; mission becomes spiritual colonialism; communication turns into propaganda, education into indoctrination, technological achievement into ecological disaster.

What can be done? There always have been those who maintain that the only thing to do is to get out, who have, as Rauschenbusch put it, 'called the world evil and left it', but that fails to take adequate account of belief in God as re-creator. If God is seen as creator of all that is, and if the fall is seen to involve the structures of society as well as individuals in it, then God's work of new creation must be understood in social as well as individualistic terms. The cross by which we are saved is also the means by which the powers are tamed and put back in their place so that their destructive force is dissipated and their creative possibilities restored.

The ground of our hope, therefore, is Jesus Christ. He too faced the powers, but, unlike the rest of us, he did not succumb either by escaping from them or by giving them final authority over him. He lived, for example, in Roman occupied territory; he benefited from the measure of law and order that Rome provided but refused to acknowledge its final authority even to save his own life. He lived within the religious framework of Judaism, honouring Law and Prophets, worshipping in Temple and synagogue, but at the crucial point where religious institutions threatened genuine love for neighbour and thus true worship of God he defied them. He healed on the Sabbath and foretold the destruction of the Temple; he lived and died a Jew and must have felt the force of the nationalist cause but did not throw in his lot with the insurrectionists. He lived his life with the knowledge of his own God-given capacity but did not use this for his own ends, refusing the temptation to stave off his own hunger, to convince himself of his calling or to make a national hero of himself.[29] The cross represents both the final temptation to serve his own ends ('come down from the cross') and the final rejection of that possibility. The double irony of the taunt of the crowd lay in its literal truth – he saved others; he could not then save himself.

This was Jesus Christ facing the powers, refusing to give them dominion over him. Here the new age was inaugurated because one had lived out his life completely under the authority of God's kingdom while within the kingdoms of this world. The evil hold of the worldly powers was broken because Jesus had faced them and not succumbed. He had not escaped, but neither had he given them final authority by using their methods, accepting their inducements or following their way of judging right and wrong. By refusing the rewards they offered, and refusing to fight them on their own terms even when facing their ultimate sanction of death[30] Jesus rendered them powerless over him and put them back in their rightful place. The cross was therefore already accomplishment, not for its own sake as some kind of ritual propitiation but because the climax of obedience to the Father and unremitting love for humankind. With the resurrection came God's vindication of *this* life as victory despite apparent defeat, the life of new creation.

(b) *Responsible action.* To believe in Jesus Christ as God's new creation, however, is not just to believe *that* this occurred but to believe *in* him who is the new creation, and that involves living in such a way that we make it real in our own time, taking our own stand and living from the perspective and with the resources it provides. This does not imply escaping from the powers, nor simply supporting them, but recognizing them when they have gone beyond bounds and showing them up for what they have become so that once again they can be used creatively and constructively. But how is this to be done? How can the powers be recognized as going beyond bounds and beginning to dominate, and what sort of action will expose them and put them back in their place?

I do not think that those questions can be answered in general terms. Answers should come as people find themselves together in particular situations and seek to know what it is there and then to be obedient to the word of new creation incarnate in Jesus Christ. Guidance from other ages and decisions of other communities are not to be neglected, but no general formulae can be given to cover all circumstances. This is not to say that no content can be given to the idea of living under the sign of the new creation; it is to say that other times and other decisions provide graphic examples, compelling illustrations and strong encouragement, but not prescriptive rules. Van den Heuvel recognized this and put forward his tests for recognizing whether the powers had over-reached themselves (Do they divide or unite? Do they focus attention on self or direct us to the needs of others? Do they claim ultimacy or are they open to amendment? Do they set us free or bind us to the past?) not as sole or final criteria but as guides that have been used and could again be useful in exposing powers for what they are and consequently breaking their destructive hold.

To sum up this approach of innovation then, it recognizes this world and the forces that shape it as God's good creation. It believes in the power of God to renew these when they become distorted and destructive. It believes in Jesus Christ as the one in whom this new creation has become a reality. It believes in our calling to reflect this recreative purpose in our own lives and in the community at large.

Such an approach looks for change all right, but does it take seriously enough the need for radical change? Many would say it does not.

4. AS REVOLUTIONARIES

The views of Richard Shaull (who, along with Moltmann,

have had formative influence on Rubem Alves referred to in the previous chapter) raise critical questions for the 'innovators' at a number of points.

Shaull is convinced, for example, that the powers that shape the world have, so to speak, joined forces.[31] They have become so powerful and all-pervasive that even the changes usually proposed by the super-powers that confront each other across the ideological gulfs are really changes within one overall interlocking complex system. Western democracies and Eastern bloc nations, for instance, have combined to provide a perspective on the world situation that has two co-ordinates – 'trust in natural harmony, with its assumption that society can move towards greater justice and fuller human life within the framework of institutional continuity'; and trust in modern technology, assumed to be the major revolutionary force of our time. Those who adopt that perspective, he says,

> do not deny the seriousness of the problems we face, but are convinced that these problems can be met and solved within given institutional structures . . . [They] are much concerned about change and innovation, but of a very specific type. It must be ordered change which can occur within the present system.[32]

Against this Shaull maintains that the christian community must sound another Barthian 'No'. Far from agreeing that this ordered change is working for the liberation of human kind, he claims that it offers only new enslavement. What is needed is a revolutionary stand that is taken up outside and over against the assumptions, presuppositions and structures of the whole system.

I caught the force of what he was saying in 1968 at the Assembly of the World Council of Churches in Uppsala. A delegate from the USA spoke in general session, extolling space exploration as a means of grasping more fully God's creative purpose and of rolling back the limits of creaturely existence. He was followed by a Russian Orthodox priest, and the Assembly waited to hear whether a 'Nyet' would be hurled at the previous speaker. On the contrary, the tone was warm and conciliatory. In such exploration, it was declared, we can see the beginnings of the fulfilment of God's purpose for the nations as they begin to work together, sharing their knowledge and co-operating for the greater good. Next came a Latin American who announced a plague on both their houses. 'You may be co-operating for your own liberation from ignorance and enmity,' he declared, 'but that works for our continued enslavement. You roll back the horizons of knowledge without rolling back the poverty and injustice in our world whose nations you keep in subjection with your equally oppressive systems.'

So, as we saw in the previous chapter, in the third world in particular theological justification for revolutionary movements has taken various forms, such as Alves' theology of messianism.[33] That God is creator means that he is no stranger to history but 'enters it and conquers it with his warfare'. Since history now displays the fallenness of man as the bondage of the oppressed, the vocation of the Messiah is to liberate those under bondage, thus giving to his kingdom a basically political character. This necessarily involves violence since the strong man's house must be broken into and he must be tied up and reduced to impotence, but use of violence in the politics of the Messiah should be seen as an instrument of love because it finally liberates master along with slave from the bondage of their unjust relationship.

Shaull himself is more restrained in his theology of revolution. He does not propose a systematic theology that justifies or demands or provides a plan for revolution, but one that gives some theological guidelines to those who find themselves in a revolutionary situation, a situation, he maintains, which exists just as much in Western countries as in Latin America or Africa, although in a different form. No longer can justice be achieved in the way advocated by

Reinhold Niebuhr, through the political realism of balancing the powers against one another in order to neutralize the effects of human egotism. Now countervailing power is rapidly giving way to the co-operation of business and labour, government and military, technology and science, even capitalism and socialism, to maintain the present over-all system. Therefore many take their stand among the revolutionaries, convinced that only this can bring about the radical change needed for human well-being and fulfilment.

What has the christian faith to offer in these circumstances? Four things, Shaull maintains. Biblical symbols and images that stress discontinuity, that picture the end of the old order and the emergence of the radically new. A theology of the cross that points to the victory hidden under apparent defeat, encouraging the revolutionary to see that his weakness is stronger than he imagined, and that persecution, suffering and defeat can contribute to eventual victory. A belief in new creation that looks for order and stability on the other side of chaos and is therefore not afraid of the spectre of anarchy since it looks for the organization of society on terms supplied not by the past but by the future. And a belief in the transcendence of the creator and the sinfulness of mankind that will not allow any revolution to become idolatrous and identify its results with Utopia.

> What this means is that Christian faith can provide resources for being authentically revolutionary . . . the type of person whose inward experience of death and resurrection equip him to let the old die when its time has come and frees him to give form to the new possibilities open to him . . . men and women liberated for creativity.[34]

This is a strong and persuasive case, but a number of considerations keep me from wholehearted endorsement.

(a) First, while this revolutionary approach begins at a different point from the one that advocates living in coalition, its hope springs from the same source – human creativity interpreted as inbuilt capacity to succeed. While the doctrine of the fall is taken seriously it is not spread widely or evenly enough, for while the fallenness of society is recognized there is a tendency to underestimate the fallenness of those working for revolutionary change. Although events may have made Niebuhr's proposal of balancing the powers outmoded, his analysis of the underlying problem of power remains valid. There is no power or authority without its self-corrupting core. The guerilla strategy that Shaull advocates, applying pressure constantly at many points to change the system rather than tearing it down all at once, may be less likely than others to absolutize the revolution. Nevertheless the revolutionary, no less than the technologist whose commitment to orderly change he criticizes, sees history as the *self*-emancipation of humanity. The technologist, as Charles West has pointed out, speaks of development and the revolutionary of liberation through confrontation. The technologist is optimistic about society's potential, the revolutionary pessimistic. But underlying that despair is still the humanist premise, 'that man is a self-liberating animal who achieves his humanity by struggling against the dehumanizing forces of nature and society, and whose self-transformation in this process is his destiny'.[35]

That, it seems to me, expects both too much and too little – too much of man who consistently turns his creative capacities to destructive ends; too little of God who comes from beyond man's own sphere of management to offer new directions and possibilities. It may reflect some of the surface imagery of struggle and conflict in which the New Testament depicts the breaking in of the new but fails to grasp the heart of the apocalyptic message, which is that the possibility of new creation cannot emerge out of anything that belongs to the stream of human history, but is brought to it from the creator who makes all things new.

(b) Second, while the revolutionary approach makes a great deal of the theme of new creation it does not make enough of the *shape* of the new creation in Jesus Christ.

Both Shaull and Alves refer to God's new creation in Jesus Christ and they use the symbols of death and resurrection as paradigms of revolutionary action – no gradual development through influencing the ruling powers but a break with the past and a radically new beginning. But while this sees Jesus as confirming the *that* of new creation, its content comes not so much from the Gospel witness to his life as from parallels in historical revolutions, past and present. Then every freedom movement is liable to be identified as the liberating work of God without measuring them against the way that Jesus chose.

However, this use of revolution as a kind of hermeneutical spotlight focusses on the 'that' of new creation while leaving the most distinctive feature of the Gospel, the form of the new creation in Jesus Christ, in the shadows. It is in the life of Jesus of Nazareth, according to the New Testament, that we see the re-creative power of God. It was through his life, obedient even to death, that the evil powers were overcome. His death and resurrection were then not just symbols of the suffering and the radical break with the past that any revolution entails; they were the culmination of his particular way of living in obedience to God and for the sake of others, and only the most speculative exegesis can avoid the conclusion that he faced the insurrectionist option as a real one, but rejected it, so that while his death was one reserved for slaves and revolutionaries, the life that led to that death was the antithesis of most political revolutionaries.[36] In fact his refusal to take the way of the zealot was part of the obedience through which the new creation became manifest. There is something fundamentally contradictory, therefore, about a christian theology of messianism which underplays the significance of *Jesus* as Messiah. He did not fulfil the role that the revolutionaries had prepared, and no attempt to live in the world as new creatures in Christ ought to overlook that fact.

This does not say all that needs to be said, of course, about christian involvement in power struggles and violence. I realize that revolutions do not usually initiate violence but are the long-suppressed reaction to the prior violence of long-term oppression and injustice, and that so-called non-violent protests often provoke violence, and do so deliberately as a technique for effecting change. Many of the great and necessary reforms of the past, such as the abolition of slavery, came about only through violent intervention, or at least involved such intervention.[37] I accept the Uppsala statement that 'some Christians will be among those who, despairing of the removal or reduction of economic injustice by peaceful means, feel obliged to have recourse to violence as a last resort'.[38] The fact remains that only a drastic reinterpretation of the New Testament can avoid the conclusion that Jesus met that kind of violence not with more of the same but with suffering love.

(c) Whatever opinion we may form of particular theologies of revolution, living as a new creation in Christ does have revolutionary effects. Neither Paul nor the other early Christian theologians developed a theology of revolution, yet their worship of the one God and their repudiation of all other aspirants, their commitment to Jesus Christ and their refusal to give allegiance to any other pretenders to the title 'Lord', had a profoundly revolutionary effect, not only in heaven but also, as Moltmann points out,[39] here on earth. By refusing to worship the Emperor or to absolutize the law of Judaism they struck at the foundations of 'political religion and religious politics'. And in our own society, worship of God the creator which thereby cuts down to size the social, political, racial, economic and national gods would bring about another revolution. Holding to Jesus Christ and his way of love as new creation, siding consistently with the poor and the oppressed, the humble and humiliated, the labouring and the overburdened, the outcast, the afflicted and dispossessed, would turn the existing order upside down.

But how is one to live with revolutionary effectiveness, looking toward an order that reflects the will of the creator-God? By finding in Jesus Christ not only the end – the liberation of humanity – but also the means by which this is finally to be achieved.

It is, of course, unfashionable to take Jesus as the norm for social ethics. Reinhold Niebuhr's contention that a socio-political policy cannot be made out of a religio-moral ideal is still widely accepted, and to question it is seen as biblically naïve, theologically inept and politically unrealistic. None of these strictures, however, ought to go unchallenged. Recent developments in biblical and theological scholarship have put the witness to Jesus' life in a new light, and the bleak outlook for the future of humanity within existing social and economic orders is forcing a reassessment of what has passed for political realism.

On the biblical front the initial shock waves set rolling by scholars who questioned whether anything could be known with objective certainty about Jesus' life and whether any of the teaching attributed to him could be counted on as his, have now died down. A new appreciation for the interpretative aspect of all history writing has tempered the most extreme scepticism about the reliability of the New Testament witness, allowing an increasing number of scholars to affirm at least the general direction that Jesus' life took, and to say that while many parts of the witness are not literal description or accurate chronology or verbatim report they do form integral components of literary-theological testimonies to the significance of Jesus. That those who told the story already believed in Jesus as Lord does not invalidate that testimony; it commits us to bring that perspective to bear as we try to understand our situation and to decide between courses of action open to us.

Theologians for their part are more ready than they were to recognize the relationship between this question of who Jesus was and the question of what we should be doing. John Yoder is one who has recently argued for the need to 'throw a cable across the chasm which usually separates the disciplines of New Testament exegesis and contemporary social ethics',[40] and while one must examine with care what he imports across that cable, his arguments against those who refuse any such link are convincing. It is simply not true that when Jesus taught and lived non-retaliation this was directed only to one-to-one relationships and is therefore irrelevant to the situations in society that confront us today. In the New Testament his life and teaching is set within the social and political context of the time, and the direction he chose consistently to take, embodying self-giving suffering love, is portrayed as running counter to the real alternative of armed insurrection. Nor can this be written off by saying that this was depicted as Jesus' way all right, but a unique way reserved for the incarnate Son of God. This is to be the way of his followers too, who are to shoulder the same cross and face the same treatment. No longer, therefore, can attempts to draw conclusions about christian social action from the attitudes of Jesus be dismissed as quietist advocacy of withdrawal from responsibility for the world. While some have used the life and teaching of Jesus to justify the extreme alienist view of the corruption of the world and to shun every possible contact with it, that is an unwarranted conclusion that results from isolating a few sayings and incidents from the rest of his life and teaching, from 'spiritualizing' the context within which the Gospel writers set the whole of his ministry,[41] and from equating his refusal to endorse any of the social power structures with a rejection of society. But his challenge to the authority of the powers was, as we have seen, no withdrawal from the world. On the contrary, it was a total involvement with the human situation and an engagement with the worldly authorities that had the most profound implications for the social, political and religious structures of the time. Consequently looking at the witness to his life as a basis for social action provides no excuse for withdrawal but a model for involvement.

This model is built not on the humanistic or sentimental illusion that we can imitate the perfection of Jesus, but on the faithful conviction that Jesus was God incarnate. This, as we saw at the end of the last chapter, is where the logic of Moltmann's argument in *The Crucified God* leads us – if the life of Jesus which culminates in the cross is the normative way of God in the world, then that must also be the way of those whose actions are sacramentally to participate in the history of God.[42] Or, to put the point in a slightly different way, if we are called to share God's re-creative work in the world then we find where that is going on by looking for actions and movements that are congruent with the way that Jesus lived and taught.

In a short but provocative essay[43] David Jenkins has also affirmed the link between the lordship of Jesus Christ and the stand of Christians in the world. What follows from the conviction that in him God was incarnate, that the resurrection confirmed that this was the life that fulfilled the purpose of God? It means, says Jenkins, that 'the ultimate power which is capable of bringing in and establishing the Kingdom of God is the love of God (the God who is love)', and that love comes to fulfilment in what the world writes off as powerlessness:

> If (and it is a big 'if'!) we are ever to get to a state of equilibrium in which all are fulfilled in each other and each can enjoy all (a creative kingdom of love) then there must be a power at work which will *absorb* powerful power rather than *counter* power with more of the same.[44]

This may not settle the question of whether Christians are ever justified in engaging in acts of violence, but it does imply that any such actions for the alleviation of injustice and oppression do not, in themselves, 'anticipate and incarnate' the presence of the creator-God in history. Sacramental involvement with the history of God[45] belongs to actions which participate in the cross of Christ, meeting violence with the suffering love that refuses to retaliate in kind, which forgives rather than condemns, looks for reconciliation with the enemy rather than his destruction, and which therefore opens the possibility of new creation.

Now this may seem so remote a promise of God's action directed to new creation that any human action shaped by it appears hopelessly idealistic, that is, without any realistic hope that such action can effect the liberation of humanity. However, the obvious breakdown of existing social, political and economic systems and their incapacity to deal with the overwhelming problems of national and racial tension, spreading poverty and famine, and destruction of the environment that gives us life, allows for a reassessment of what is really realistic. 'More of the same' leads to death if the prescription was the wrong one in the first place. Power exercised as it is by the worldly authorities does, as Jenkins points out, always involve counter-action and counter-effects, and the 'christian realism' of Niebuhr and others who advocated power-balancing now seems to be far from realistic at either national or international level. Once we have recognized the endless convolutions of human power-seeking, the frightening escalation involved in keeping the balance between super-powers and the certain capacity for immediate or protracted self-destruction, is it so unrealistic to base hope on a revolution more radical than any other, one that disarms the worldly powers by refusing their terms for the exercise of power?

Such, according to Moltmann, was the revolution of Jesus, the 'humane revolt'[46] which began with the revolutionary proclamation of the grace of God to sinners, which continued in a life that steadfastly resisted the temptation of falling victim to the 'vicious circle of legalism, of violence and counter-violence, of guilt or retribution',[47] which came to its climax in a death inevitably provoked by such a radical rejection of the ultimacy of the worldly powers of religion and state, and which is seen not as the end of hope but as its beginning through the resurrection of Jesus from the dead.

What troubles me most about this conclusion is not that it appears unrealistic but that it can seem detached and uncaring, an easy option for one who is not suffering, as so many are, under the sustained violence of injustice and oppression. It would, of course, be intolerable for us to sit in judgement over those in desperate situations who see things differently and feel impelled to violent reaction, but two considerations may enable us still to point to the perspective offered by the cross. First, there are at least some Christians in those situations whose costly involvement is beyond dispute and who also see the way of the cross as the way of obedience that holds out the only real hope of the future. Helder Camara in South America is one; C. F. Beyers Naudé, recently under fire from the All Africa Conference of Churches as well as from the South African Government for his consistent advocacy of change through non-violent means, is another. Second, to follow this way must not be seen as an alternative to action, a do-nothing stand in which we remain aloof and call on others to do the suffering. It means finding ways of identifying in our situation with the poor and oppressed in theirs. In Australia, for example, it means standing against and refusing to profit from the counterparts in our own society of the institutions and forces that keep other people poor. It means facing and exposing the powers in our own midst, showing up and denouncing the racial violence that has been with us ever since white people arrived, giving up the use of power as a means of self-aggrandisement, renouncing the right to gain and keep all we can for ourselves, thus releasing our resources and capacities for the wider benefit of the whole of humanity.

Will it be said then that the Christians are absent from the world? Curious that 'presence in the world' should mean accepting the world's ways, means, objectives; should mean helping hate and evil to proliferate! Christians will be sufficiently and completely present in the world if they suffer with those who suffer, if they seek out with those sufferers the one way of salvation, if they bear witness before God and man to the consequences of injustice and the proclamation of love. (Jacques Ellul)[48]

Notes

1. Almost certainly because the controversies that gave rise to them involved the doctrine of creation. In those early days the challenge to the integrity of the faith came from two sides, from the Gnostics who tended to merge Christianity with other religious systems, and, from the opposite quarter, those who affirmed the absolute uniqueness of Christianity and so its discontinuity with Judaism. Both of these had distinctive views of creation. The Gnostics usually held to some form of emanation theory which saw the world as spun out of the being of God. Marcion, according to his critics, maintained that the world was created by the God of darkness who was other than, and finally defeated by, the God and Father of Jesus Christ. In the face of these challenges the Church affirmed a view of creation that stood over against both – one God, creator of the world and Father of Jesus Christ, who brought into being a world that was other than himself.

2. Although the work comprises only four volumes, each of the volumes was published in at least two separate part-volumes, and one of these part-volumes has a first and second half also published separately.

3. Claus Westermann maintains that the variety of biblical witness itself precludes any assertion about 'the biblical witness' to how the world began. He identifies a number of different traditions in the Old Testament that have been put side by side without any attempt to reconcile them, or to give priority to one or the other. 'The process of Creation has not been and cannot be established definitively: each age can only express it in a way intelligible to itself' (Claus Westermann, *Creation*, trans. J. J. Scullion (SPCK, London, and Fortress Press, Philadelphia, 1974), p. 5).

4. 'The Churches defended against the natural sciences a teaching on Creation which did not in its essential points correspond to the biblical reflection on Creator-Creation' (ibid., p. 4).

5. A phrase coined by Professor A. Boyce Gibson of Melbourne to describe the *détente* between Barthians and Logical Positivists in the 1950s who agreed, although for very different reasons, that philosophical discussion of God was futile.

6. Among the most thorough-going expositions of this view is that found in Carl Michalson's *The Rationality of Faith* (Scribner's, New York, 1963, and SCM Press, London, 1964).

7. Strongly affirmed, for example, in Bonhoeffer's radio broadcast entitled 'The Idea of Leader in the New Germany', cut off the air before completion.

8. Arend van Leeuwen, *Christianity in World History* (Edinburgh House, London, 1964).

9. Lynn White, Jr, 'The Historical Roots of our Ecological Crisis', in *Science*, vol. 155, March 1967, pp. 1203 ff.

10. John Macquarrie, 'Creation and Environment', in *Expository Times*, October 1971, pp. 4 ff.

2. CREATION AND GENESIS

1. For an assessment of some conflicting views of the origin of one major theme in the tradition, see E. W. Nicholson, *Exodus and Sinai in History and Tradition* (Blackwell's, Oxford, 1973).

2. G. von Rad, *Genesis* (SCM Press, London, 1961), p. 149.

3. As B. W. Anderson notes in his *Creation versus Chaos* (Association Press, New York, 1967).

4. Westermann, op. cit., pp. 12–13.

5. In chapters 2 and 3 of his *Creation*, Westermann shows the way the authors are 'on the one hand the preservers of the old traditions, and on the other the proclaimers of a new message in a new age' (p. 30).

6. J. Burnet, *Early Greek Philosophy* (A. & C. Black, London, 1908), p. 6. Burnet goes on to say that their systematizing did not meet the needs of many, hence the later revival of more primitive religious expressions in, especially, the Orphic religion from the north, with its components of revelation, community and ecstasy.

7. cf. Anderson, op. cit., p. 39.

8. M. Eliade, *Cosmos and History: The Myth of the Eternal Return* (Harper, New York, and Routledge & Kegan Paul, London, 1954), p. 56. Cited in Anderson, op. cit., p. 29.

9. Following Artur Weiser, *Psalms* (SCM Press, London, 1962), pp. 233 ff.

10. *Creation versus Chaos*, pp. 124–6.

11. Westermann, op. cit., pp. 17 ff.

12. G. S. Hendry, 'The Eclipse of Creation', in *Theology Today*, January 1972, pp. 406 ff.

13. ibid., p. 409.

14. One of the few points at which I would take issue with John Reumann in his *Creation and New Creation* (Augsburg, Minneapolis, 1973)

is this over-emphasis on the subjugation of creation to redemption themes in the Old Testament.

15. G. van der Leeuw, *Religion in Essence and Manifestation* (Harper, New York, 1963, and Allen & Unwin, London, 1964), p. 391. Cited by Anderson, op. cit., p. 118.

16. Cited by Macquarrie, op. cit., p. 6.

17. ibid., pp. 4 ff.

18. *Gates of Prayer, The New Union Prayer Book* (Central Conference of American Rabbis, New York, 1972), pp. 10-11.

3. CREATION AND FALL

1. Albert Camus, *The Plague*, trans. S. Gilbert (Hamish Hamilton, London, 1948), pp. 91–2; (Knopf, New York, 1952), pp. 87–8.

2. D. Bonhoeffer, *Creation and Fall* (SCM Press, London, and Macmillan, New York, 1959), pp. 74–5, 78.

3. See especially Lynn White, Jr's essay, op. cit.

4. For a summary of the ways in which the Church's theology has indirectly encouraged exploitation, see B. E. Santmire, *Brother Earth: Nature, God and Ecology in a Time of Crisis* (Nelson, New York, 1970), pp. 66 ff.

5. *kabash*, trample; *radah*, tread. Both also used metaphorically to imply subjugation.

6. Bonhoeffer, op. cit., p. 44.

7. In an address entitled 'Ecological Commitment as Theological Responsibility', delivered in St Xavier's College, Chicago, in January 1970.

8. D. Bonhoeffer, *Letters and Papers from Prison*, enlarged ed. (SCM Press, London, and Macmillan, New York, 1971), p. 360.

9. R. Gregor Smith, *Secular Christianity* (Collins, London, 1966).

10. H. R. Niebuhr, *Radical Monotheism and Western Culture* (Harper, New York, 1960, and Faber & Faber, London, 1961).

11. *Radical Monotheism*, p. 27.

12. ibid., p. 28.

13. 1 Cor. 15:23.

14. From a comment by Erich Fromm, reported in *In Unity*, vol. 13, no. 4, June 1966.

15. Albert Camus, *The Fall* (Hamish Hamilton, London, 1957), p. 16; (Knopf, New York, 1956), pp. 18–19.

16. ibid., pp. 37, 63, 76; pp. 48, 84, 102.

17. The theme of Reinhold Niebuhr's Gifford Lectures, *Moral Man and Immoral Society* (Scribner's, London, 1946).

18. In this capitalism and communism are, as Emil Brunner once put it, 'twin brothers' (Gifford Lectures for 1947), for they are both born of economic totalitarianism. Members of the third world now agree.

19. Jürgen Moltmann, *Religion, Revolution and the Future* (Scribner's, New York, 1969), pp. 183–4.

4. CREATION AND NEW CREATION

1. In his essay, 'What is New in Christianity?', published in *Religion, Revolution and the Future*. The direction which this present chapter takes is largely a response to Moltmann's article.

2. J. Reumann, op. cit., pp. 57–82.

3. B. W. Anderson, op. cit., p. 109.

4. The term used is the same as in Gen. 1:1.

5. Moltmann, op. cit., p. 8.

6. B. A. Santmire in his *Brother Earth* lists passages which indicate how the expectation of new creation involves the natural world. However, he tends to over-emphasize the significance of some of these by failing to recognize that many of the references to nature do little more than set the stage either for the people's release and the 'long march' (Isa. 43) or for their future well-being (Joel 2:18–23). The redemption of the people remains paramount. Westermann is more discriminating in his use of the texts, but still concludes that although references to the end are at first scattered, they 'take on steadily increasing significance and scope' until finally in Isaiah 'the salvation that has been announced to the people of God is made universal, and the nations, the world and nature, especially the animals, are included in the picture' (*Beginning and End* (Fortress Press, Philadelphia, 1972), pp. 18, 19).

7. Initially this probably reflected expectation for this age, the result in history of a government under a wise leader who would come from the family of Jesse. But in later Jewish tradition and Christian understanding this becomes part of the expectation of events at the end of the age which will inaugurate the new.

8. Mark 4:41.

9. Mark 6:52.

10. W. D. Davies, *Paul and Rabbinic Judaism* (SPCK, London, 1948), comments: 'We cannot doubt that in Mk. 4:35–41 and 5:1–20 the incarnation is thought of as new creation' (p. 41).

11. He must have elaborated on this further in an unpublished lecture (see Anderson, op. cit., pp. 162–3).

12. See, for example, M. Black, 'The Pauline Doctrine of the Second Adam', in *Scottish Journal of Theology*, June 1954, p. 170.

13. This represents a projection from present experience back to the beginning, parallel to Israel's projection of historical experience of Yahweh back to the beginning of things.

14. C. Westermann, *Beginning and End*, p. 19. >

15. Moltmann, op. cit., pp. 10 ff.

16. A phrase associated especially with H. Gunkel.

17. Moltmann, op. cit., pp. 35-36.

18. See my note on Bultmann's exegetical procedure, *History and Existential Theology* (Epworth Press, London, and Westminster Press, Philadelphia, 1969), pp. 51–5.

19. See Westermann, *Beginning and End*, pp. 33–9.

20. C. F. D. Moule, *Man and Nature in the New Testament* (Athlone Press, London, 1964).

21. J. Reumann, op. cit., p. 99.

5. TRANSCENDENTALIST: KARL BARTH

1. Karl Barth, *The Humanity of God* (John Knox Press, Richmond, Va, 1960, and Collins, London, 1961), p. 41.

2. ibid., pp. 40, 41.

3. K. Barth, *Credo* (Hodder & Stoughton, London, 1936), p. 30.

4. *The Humanity of God*, p. 40.

5. 'It is therefore not . . . that the world is by nature God's child. Nor is it that the world is to be understood as an outflow, an emanation from God, as something divine which wells out of God like a stream out of a spring. That would really not be creation, but a living movement of God, an expression of Himself. But creation means something different; it means a reality distinct from God' (*Dogmatics in Outline* (SCM Press, London, 1949), pp. 54–5).

6. Consequently Barth was claimed as a theological ancestor by some of the 'secular theologians' of the 1960s, notably van Buren and Hamilton.

7. Carl Michalson used Pascal in expounding his view of the hiddenness of God ('The Real Presence of the Hidden God', in *Faith and Ethics*, ed. Paul Ramsey (Harper, New York, 1957), pp. 245–8).

8. Cf. Rudolf Otto, *The Idea of the Holy* (Oxford University Press, London, 1936).

9. *Credo*, p. 30.

10. *Dogmatics in Outline*, pp. 50, 52.

11. ibid., p. 54.

12. *Credo*, p. 20.

13. *Day by Day We Magnify Thee*, ed M. Steiner and P. Scott (Epworth Press, London, and Muhlenberg, Philadelphia, 1950), p. 27.

14. 'It is of a piece with the nature of evil that if we could explain how it may have reality it would not be evil' (*Church Dogmatics*, vol. IV, part 3, first half (T. & T. Clark, Edinburgh, and Scribner's, New York, 1961), p. 177).

15. Not that man once *possessed* the image of God which has now been destroyed (cf. the Brunner-Barth controversy about the *imago dei*), but that what fallen men and women do 'is no doubt a denial of their divine image and likeness, and laden with all the mortal sickness which is a consequence of this denial' (*Church Dogmatics*, vol. III, part 1 (T. & T. Clark, Edinburgh, and Scribner's, New York, 1958), p. 191). Still the creator maintains his relationship with mankind, and although man may have turned the blessing of this into curse, he still 'has reason to look for the man who will be . . . real man for him, in the image and likeness of God . . . namely, Jesus Christ and His community' (ibid., p. 190).

16. K. Barth, *The Epistle to the Romans* (Oxford University Press, London, 1932), pp. 177, 168.

17. *Church Dogmatics*, vol. IV, part 1 (T. & T. Clark, Edinburgh, and Scribner's, New York, 1956), ch. XIV.

18. 'Church and Culture', in *Theology and Church* (SCM Press, London, and Harper & Row, New York, 1962), p. 348.

19. ibid.

20. Cited by Will Herberg in his introductory essay in *Community, State and Church* (Anchor Books, New York, 1960), p. 23.

21. *Theology and Church*, p. 349.

22. e.g. Herberg, op. cit.

23. J. Moltmann, *The Crucified God* (SCM Press, London, and Harper & Row, New York, 1974), p. 72.

24. Barth, *Romans*, p. 310.

25. *Die kirchliche Dogmatik*, vol. III, part 4, p. 376n.; cited and translated by Paul Santmire in his doctoral thesis 'Creation and Nature' (Harvard, 1966), p. 125.

26. Paul Santmire, in a section of his doctoral thesis (op. cit.) which was not published with the rest in *Brother Earth*, points to the ironical fact that Barth who attacked anthropocentrism in the doctrine of God and man succumbed to it in his doctrine of nature, even giving it dogmatic support and leaving himself with a non-theological mechanistic view of nature, akin to that of scientific humanism.

6. ONTOLOGICAL: PAUL TILLICH

1. In *The Interpretation of History* (Scribner's, New York, 1936), he indicates his debt to German Idealism, and says that he is an idealist if this means 'the assertion of the identity of thinking and being as the principle of truth' (p. 61). This in turn goes back to its origins in Plato and neo-Platonism.

2. P. Tillich, *Systematic Theology*, vol. 1 (Nisbet, London, 1953), p. 68; (University of Chicago Press, Chicago, 1951), p. 60.

3. ibid., p. 77; p. 68.

4. ibid., p. 187; p. 168.

5. ibid., p. 189; p. 170.

6. ibid., p. 189; p. 171.

7. ibid., p. 190; p. 172.

8. ibid., p. 193; p. 174.

9. ibid., p. 280; p. 252.

10. ibid.

11. ibid., p. 281; p. 253.

12. ibid., p. 291; p. 262.

13. ibid.

14. ibid., p. 293; p. 264.

15. ibid., p. 296; pp. 266–7.

16. ibid., pp. 287–8; p. 259.

17. P. Tillich, *The Dynamics of Faith* (Allen & Unwin, London, 1957), p. 112.

18. *Systematic Theology*, vol. 3 (Nisbet, London, 1964), p. 427; (University of Chicago Press, Chicago, 1963), p. 401

19. *Systematic Theology*, vol. 2 (Nisbet, London, 1957), p. 112; (University of Chicago Press, Chicago, 1951), p. 97.

20. ibid., p. 137; p. 119.

21. ibid., p. 159; p. 138.

22. ibid., p. 137; p. 119.

23. ibid.

24. e.g. K. Hamilton, *The System and the Gospel* (SCM Press, London, 1963).

25. Barth's own aphorism in *The Humanity of God*, p. 43.

26. op. cit., where God remains 'absolutely superior'.

27. *Systematic Theology*, vol. 1, p. 40; p. 35.

28. Although not itself a biblical term.

29. *Systematic Theology*, vol. 1, p. 208; pp. 188–9.

30. ibid., p. 280; p. 252.

31. Most recently, with Carl Braaten in *Christ and Counter-Christ* (Fortress Press, Philadelphia, 1972).

32. P. Tillich, *The Future of Religions* (Harper, New York, 1966), p. 69.

33. op. cit.

34. ibid., p. 6.

35. *Systematic Theology*, vol. 1, p. 280; p. 252.

36. Michael Moore, in an unpublished essay, 'Christian Faith and Environmental Crisis in the Theology of Paul Tillich' (New Haven, 1974), has demonstrated this.

37. *Systematic Theology*, vol. 3, p. 224; p. 210.

38. ibid., pp. 436, 432; pp. 409, 405.

7. EXISTENTIALIST: RUDOLF BULTMANN

1. Some critics of existentialism define it in these terms too, and then go on to reject all forms on that score.

2. R. Bultmann, *Glauben und Verstehen*, vol. 1 (Mohr, Tübingen, 1933), pp. 36–7.

3. R. Bultmann, *History and Eschatology* (Edinburgh University Press, Edinburgh, 1957), p. 141.

4. R. Bultmann, *Jesus Christ and Mythology* (Scribner's, New York, 1958, and SCM Press, London, 1960), p. 69.

5. R. Bultmann, *Existence and Faith* (Living Age, New York, 1960, and Hodder & Stoughton, London, 1961), p. 177.

6. 'Faith in God the Creator' (1934).

7. *Existence and Faith*, p. 174.

8. Cited by Carl Michalson in *Faith for Personal Crises* (Scribner's, New York, 1958, and Epworth Press, London, 1959).

9. *Existence and Faith*, p. 179.

10. Bultmann uses Heidegger's term, but with some modifications in connotation. See J. Macquarrie, *An Existentialist Theology* (SCM Press, London, 1955), and N. J. Young, op. cit., pp. 135–41.

11. Bultmann uses Heidegger's analysis of the human condition, appropriating the headings of 'anxiety', 'care' and 'death'.

12. *History and Eschatology*, p. 150.

13. R. Bultmann, *Theology of the New Testament*, vol. I (Scribner's, New York, 1951, and SCM Press, London, 1965), p. 255.

14. R. Bultmann, *Kerygma and Myth*, vol. I (SPCK, London, 1953), p. 31.

15. ibid., p. 32.

16. From those who wish that he had been more thorough-going in

his demythologizing, to those who think that an inconsistent refusal to do so is all that keeps him within the orbit of Christianity.

17. *Kerygma and Myth*, vol. I, p. 37.

18. *The Listener*, September 1955, p. 360.

19. *Kerygma and Myth*, vol. I, p. 32.

20. *The Listener*, p. 361.

21. R. Bultmann, *Essays: Philosophical and Theological* (SCM Press, London, 1955), pp. 110, 289; *Kerygma and Myth*, vol. I, pp. 20, 21; *Theology of the New Testament*, vol. I, p. 19.

22. *Essays*, p. 154.

23. *Kerygma and Myth*, vol. I, p. 20.

24. A point made by Gerald O'Collins in an unpublished lecture given at Queen's College, Melbourne, in 1969.

25. R. Bultmann, *Primitive Christianity in its Contemporary Setting* (Living Age, New York, and Thames & Hudson, London, 1956), p. 92.

26. *Existence and Faith*, p. 182.

27. R. Bultmann, *Jesus and the Word* (Fontana, London, 1962), p. 11; (Scribner's, New York, 1958), p. 3.

28. Because, according to Bultmann, it is only within the context of historical decision that man can find himself.

29. e.g. John Macquarrie, Joseph Sittler, Lynn White, Jr.

30. In his reply to Paul Minear in C. Kegley, *The Theology of Rudolf Bultmann* (SCM Press, London, 1966), pp. 266–7.

31. John Reumann's phrase in *Creation and New Creation*, p. 99.

8. ESCHATOLOGICAL: JÜRGEN MOLTMANN

1. J. Moltmann, *Theology of Hope* (SCM Press, London, 1967).

2. e.g. collections of essays published in *Religion, Revolution and the Future* and *Hope and Planning* (SCM Press, London, 1971).

3. Reinhold Niebuhr, *Does Civilization Need Religion?* (Macmillan, New York, 1928), p. 12.

4. R. Bultmann, *The Listener*, September 1955, p. 358.

5. J. Moltmann, *Theology of Hope*, p. 21.

6. *Religion, Revolution and the Future*, p. 139.

7. Barth, *Romans*, p. 314; cited by Moltmann, *Theology of Hope*, p. 39.

8. *Religion, Revolution and the Future*, pp. 35, 36.

9. Mircea Eliade, op. cit.

10. *Religion, Revolution and the Future*, p. 60.

11. *The Crucified God*, pp. 271–5.

12. *Theology of Hope*, p. 22.

13. Following Joseph Pieper, whom he quotes in *Theology of Hope*, p. 23.

14. J. Moltmann, *Man* (SPCK, London, 1974), p. 107.

15. *Religion, Revolution and the Future*, pp. 183–4.

16. *The Crucified God*, p. 331.

17. ibid.

18. *Theology of Hope*, p. 23.

19. ibid., p. 221.

20. *The Crucified God*, p. 256.

21. His two major works are *A Theology of Human Hope* (Corpus Books, New York, 1969) and *Tomorrow's Child* (Harper & Row, New York, and SCM Press, London, 1972).

22. *A Theology of Human Hope*, p. 129.

23. ibid., pp. 107-8.

24. *Tomorrow's Child*, pp. 4-5.

25. *A Theology of Human Hope*, p. 116.

26. ibid., pp. 113, 132.

27. ibid., p. 143.

28. Especially in *Religion, Revolution and the Future*.

29. *The Crucified God*, p. 5.

30. See especially the chapters on 'The Eschatological Trial of Jesus' and 'The Crucified God', where Moltmann sets the discussion consistently in the context of Trinitarian theology.

31. *The Crucified God*, p. 277.

32. 'The cross is the beginning of the trinitarian history of God' (*The Crucified God*, p. 278).

33. ibid., p. 321.

9. LIVING IN THE CREATED WORLD

1. According to Jainism, forerunner of both Buddhism and Hinduism, any form of works necessarily binds people to the round of reincarnation, but in later versions it is desire or the attitude of dependence rather than works as such that constitutes *karma*, tying people to the earth.

2. Babylonian, Egyptian and Greek had this in common.

3. See especially Plato's myth of the cave in *The Republic*.

4. Especially the first letter of John, Ephesians 2, Romans 8.

5. AD 197–222.

6. So his famous Athens-Jerusalem opposition, philosophy seen as a counter to faith and the source of heresy.

7. *De Spectaculus*, ii; cited in H. R. Niebuhr, *Christ and Culture*, p. 53.

8. *Apologeticum*, xxi.

9. 'On Idolatry', in *Library of Christian Classics*, vol. V (SCM Press, London, and Westminster Press, Philadelphia, 1956), p. 107.

10. ibid., p. 105.

11. ibid., pp. 102–3.

12. ibid., p. 78.

13. Raynor Johnson, formerly Master of Queen's College, Melbourne, has written a number of books on spiritualism and related topics.

14. D. and N. Jackson, *Living Together in a World Falling Apart* (Creation House, Illinois, 1974), p. 66.

15. ibid., p. 67.

16. Although this criticism does have particular force against those who maintain that by living as aliens they *can* avoid the tension.

17. J. Moltmann, *The Crucified God*, p. 24.

18. cf. the views of John Yoder, *The Politics of Jesus* (Eerdmans, Grand Rapids, 1972) and William Stringfellow, *An Ethic for Christians and Other Aliens in a Strange Land* (Word, Waco, 1973).

19. G. W. F. Hegel, *The Philosophy of History* (Dover, New York, 1956), p. 72.

20. ibid., p. 39.

21. Not that they simply endorsed government policy; they usually did not. They did, however, tend to identify the kingdom of God with the culmination of human movements for social reform.

22. William Hamilton, in *Radical Theology and the Death of God* (Bobbs-Merrill, New York, 1966, and Pelican, Harmondsworth, 1968), p. 168.

23. John Yoder, op. cit., p. 101.

24. ibid.

25. e.g. in *Religion, Revolution and the Future*, p. 34.

26. R. Bultmann, essays on creation in *Existence and Faith*; H. Berkhof, *Christ and the Powers* (Herald, Scottsdale, 1962); A. van den Heuvel, *These Rebellious Powers* (SCM Press, London, 1966).

27. R. Bultmann, *Existence and Faith*, p. 205.

28. op cit., p. 145.

29. The primary strand of meaning in the temptations narrative, too quickly bypassed by commentators in favour of the symbolic meaning of the alternative ways of fulfilling the Messianic role, was that they were temptations to use his power for his own benefit – to feed himself, to reassure himself, to establish himself in the eyes of the people.

30. Stringfellow, op. cit., insists that death is the ultimate weapon of all the 'powers'.

31. R. Shaull, 'Theology and the Transformation of Society', in

Theology Today, April 1968, pp. 23 ff.

32. R. Shaull, 'Christian Faith as Scandal in a Technocratic World', in *New Theology*, no. 6, ed. M. E. Marty and D. G. Peerman (Macmillan, New York, and Collier-Macmillan, London, 1969), pp. 124-5.

33. R. Alves, *A Theology of Human Hope*.

34. R. Shaull, 'Christian Faith as Scandal', p. 131.

35. Charles West, 'Theological Guidelines for the Future', in *Theology Today*, vol. 27, no. 3, October 1970, p. 280.

36. For a recent discussion of this, see O. Cullman, *Jesus and the Revolutionaries* (Harper & Row, New York, 1970).

37. A major factor in ending the slave traffic was the public exposure in England of the horrors of slavery and subsequent pressure on the pillars of society who were profiting from it. But even when public opinion was aroused and political action taken, considerable violence still occurred before it finally ended.

38. Statement on Economic Justice and World Order, from the World Council of Churches Assembly, Uppsala, 1968. This is not to accept the argument that violence which is wrong in the hands of the oppressor is necessarily right when used to redress oppression.

39. J. Moltmann, *Religion, Revolution and the Future*, p. 137.

40. J. Yoder, op. cit., pp. 13–14.

41. It is now a commonplace to draw attention to the down-to-earth framework in which the Gospels set the ministry of Jesus, e.g. the revolutionary overtones of the Magnificat, the material promise of good news to the poor, the political alternatives of kingship faced in the temptations.

42. J. Moltmann, *The Crucified God*, p. 337.

43. 'The Power of the Powerless', written when the author was Director of Humanum Studies at Geneva. *In Search of a Theology of Development* (Sodepax Report, Geneva, 1970).

44. ibid.

45. J. Moltmann, *The Crucified God*, p. 337.

46. ibid., p. 142.

47. ibid.

48. Jacques Ellul, 'Violence', in *A Reader in Political Theology*, ed. A. Kee (SCM Press, London, 1974), p. 151.

Acknowledgements

The author would like to acknowledge his gratitude to Westminster Press for permission to include, in section 5(b) of chapter 7, material which first appeared in his *History and Existential Theology*; and to the editors of *Colloquium* for permission to include, in an amended form, some material which first appeared in his article 'Revolution as a Hermeneutical Principle' (vol. 7, no. 2, May 1975); and to the publishers for permission to quote from the following books: *Theology and Church* by Karl Barth, translated by Louise Pettibone Smith, published by SCM Press, London, and Harper & Row, New York; *Existence and Faith* by Rudolf Bultmann, translated by Schubert M. Ogden, published by Hodder & Stoughton, London, and Living Age, New York; *The Fall* by Albert Camus, translated by Justin O'Brien, copyright © 1957 by Albert Camus, Hamish Hamilton Limited, published by Hamish Hamilton, London, and Alfred A. Knopf, Inc., New York; *The Crucified God* by Jürgen Moltmann, translated by R. A. Wilson and J. Bowden, published by SCM Press, London, and Harper & Row, New York; *Religion, Revolution and the Future* by Jürgen Moltmann, translated by M. Douglas Meeks, published by Charles Scribner's Sons, New York; The New English Bible, 2nd edition © 1970 by permission of Oxford and Cambridge University Presses; and *Systematic Theology* by Paul Tillich, © University of Chicago, published by Nisbet, London, and the University of Chicago Press, Chicago.

Index

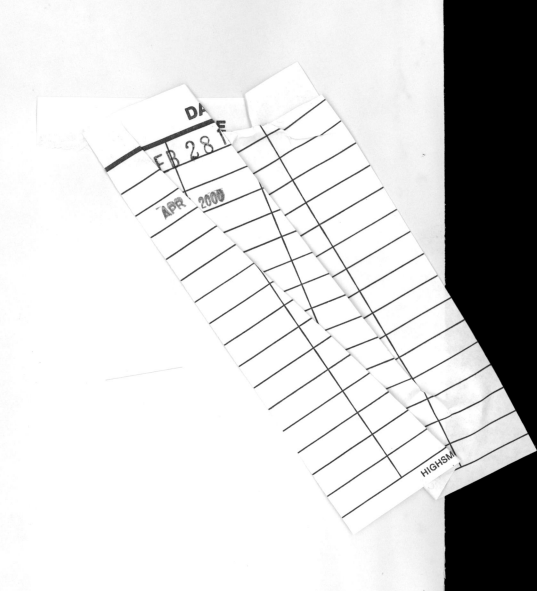